D0032915

The Curse of Bigness
Antitrust in the New Gilded Age

COLUMBIA GLOBAL REPORTS
NEW YORK

The Curse of Bigness
Antitrust in the New Gilded Age

Tim Wu

The Curse of Bigness
Antitrust in the New Gilded Age
Copyright © 2018 by Tim Wu
All rights reserved

Published by Columbia Global Reports
91 Claremont Avenue, Suite 515
New York, NY 10027
globalreports.columbia.edu
facebook.com/columbiaglobalreports
@columbiaGR

Library of Congress Control Number: 2018949786
ISBN: 978-0-9997454-6-5
E-book ISBN: 978-0-9997454-7-2

Book design by Strick&Williams
Map design by Jeffrey L. Ward
Author photograph by Miranda Sita

Printed in the United States of America

The Curse of Bigness
Antitrust in the New
Gilded Age

United States

European
Union

© 2018 Jeffrey L. Ward

For Richard Posner, who taught me to think without fear.

CONTENTS

14
Introduction

24
Chapter One
The Monopolization Movement

33
Chapter Two
The Right to Live, and Not Merely
to Exist

45
Chapter Three
The Trustbuster

78
Chapter Four
Peak Antitrust and the Chicago
School

93
Chapter Five
The Last of the Big Cases

102
Chapter Six
Chicago Triumphant

119
Chapter Seven
The Rise of the Tech Trusts

127
Conclusion
A Neo-Brandeisian Agenda

141
Acknowledgments

143
Further Reading

147
Notes

Introduction

We are four decades into a major political and economic experiment. What happens when the United States and other major nations weaken their laws meant to control the size of industrial giants? What is the impact of allowing unrestricted growth of concentrated private power, and abandoning most curbs on anticompetitive conduct?

The answers, I think, are plain. We have managed to recreate both the economics and politics of a century ago—the first Gilded Age—and remain in grave danger of repeating more of the signature errors of the twentieth century. As that era has taught us, extreme economic concentration yields gross inequality and material suffering, feeding an appetite for nationalistic and extremist leadership. Yet, as if blind to the greatest lessons of the last century, we are going down the same path. If we learned one thing from the Gilded Age, it should have been this: The road to fascism and dictatorship is paved with failures of economic policy to serve the needs of the general public.

Look at the global economy and witness the rule of concentrated oligopolies and monopolies, in industries like finance,
media, airlines, and telecommunications, just to name the most
obvious—firms whose size allows them to treat customers and
competitors with impunity. Most visible in our daily lives is
the great power of the tech platforms, especially Google, Facebook, and Amazon, who have gained extraordinary power over
our lives. With this centralization of private power has come a
renewed concentration of wealth, and a wide gap between the
rich and poor.

The concentration of wealth and power has helped transform and radicalize electoral politics. As in the Gilded Age, a
disaffected and declining middle class has come to support radically anti-corporate and nationalist candidates, catering to
a discontent that transcends party lines. A renewed economic
nationalism around the world blames immigrant workers, foreign products, or elite conspiracies for the diminishment of the
middle class. There is widespread anger at big business and how
they treat customers, especially in concentrated or monopolized industries like insurance, pharmaceuticals, airlines, and
other insensitive behemoths. Many fear Google, Amazon, and
Facebook, and their power over not just commerce, but over
politics, the news, and our private information.

What we must realize is that, once again, we face what Louis
Brandeis called the "Curse of Bigness," which, as he warned, represents a profound threat to democracy itself. What else can one
say about a time when we simply accept that industry will have
far greater influence over elections and lawmaking than mere
citizens? When the American pharmaceutical industry can raise
prices by thousands of percent, confident that government will

16   do little or nothing? Where the middle class has no apparent influence on policies like health insurance, taxes, working conditions, housing, or other matters that determine how life is really lived?

We must now face questions that have been ignored for more than a generation. Are extreme levels of industrial concentration actually compatible with the premise of rough equality among citizens, industrial freedom, or democracy itself? Can we create broad-based wealth and a sense of entrepreneurial opportunity in an economy dominated by monopolists? Is there just too much concentrated private power in too few hands, with too much influence over government and our lives?

The questions, I think, answer themselves. The main goal of this short volume is to see how the classic antidote to bigness—the antitrust and other antimonopoly laws—might be recovered and updated to face the challenges of our times. For roughly a century, the antitrust law served in practice and theory as an antimonopoly code that sought to limit excessive industrial concentration and to police monopoly conduct. By the midpoint of the last century, antitrust became widely understood in the Western world as a necessary part of a functioning democracy, as an ultimate check on private power.

Yet over the span of a generation, the law has shrunk to a shadow of itself, and somehow ceased to have a decisive opinion on the core concern of monopoly. The law that the Supreme Court once called a "comprehensive charter of economic liberty aimed at preserving free and unfettered competition" no longer condemns monopoly, but has grown ambivalent, and

sometimes even celebrates the monopolist—as if the "anti" in
"antitrust" has been discarded.

Most of what follows can be understood to center on the recovery of one principle: that in enacting and repeatedly fortifying the antitrust laws the United States made a critical, indeed Constitutional choice in industrial and national policy. After a period of intense national debate, including a presidential election in 1912 where economic policy was a central issue, the nation rejected a monopolized economy and chose repeatedly over the decades to preserve its tradition of an open and competitive market. The goal of antitrust law must be understood as respecting that choice. Or as Louis Brandeis, the great prophet of a decentralized economy, put it, the antitrust laws answered a question: "Shall the industrial policy of America be that of competition or that of monopoly?"

What happened? The law is currently suffering from an overindulgence in the ideas first popularized by Robert Bork and others at the University of Chicago over the 1970s. Bork contended, implausibly, that the Congress of 1890 exclusively intended the antitrust law to deal with one very narrow type of harm: higher prices to consumers. That theory, the "consumer welfare" approach, has enfeebled the law. Promising greater certainty and scientific rigor, it has delivered neither, and more importantly discarded far too much of the role that law was intended to play in a democracy, namely, constraining the accumulation of unchecked private power and preserving economic liberty. Forty years ago, the famed Robert Pitofsky warned that it is "bad history, bad policy, and bad law to exclude certain political values in interpreting the antitrust laws." He was right.

18   Antitrust has fallen into hibernation before as ideologies have shifted, only to come roaring back to meet the needs of the age. To deliver on its mandate, American antitrust needs both to return to its broader goals and upgrade its capacities. It needs better tools to assess new forms of market power, to assess macroeconomic arguments, and to take seriously the link between industrial concentration and political influence. It needs to take advantage of all that economics and other social sciences have to offer. It needs stronger remedies, including a return to breakups, that are designed with the broader goals of antitrust in mind. Finally, it needs to put courts back in the business of policing what Brandeis termed as conduct meant to "suppress or even destroy competition.

The alternative is not appealing. Over the twentieth century, nations that failed to control private power and attend to the economic needs of their citizens faced the rise of strongmen who promised their citizens a more immediate deliverance from economic woes. The rise of a paramount leader of government who partners with monopolized industry has an indelible association with fascism and authoritarianism. It is true that antitrust alone will not cure the curse of bigness or eliminate the excesses of private power. But it strikes at the root, and getting the engines of the law restarted is an important part of dealing with a problem that has reached Constitutional dimensions.

As such, this book is far less radical than it might be. It is actually a call for a middle path, to control economic structure before it controls us. It does not see antitrust as degraded beyond redemption, nor label its practitioners as unprofessional or untalented. It claims, rather, that the law has lost sight of its goals and has subsequently failed in its core mission. The initiatives I propose may combine to go far toward reinvigorating antitrust in our era, restoring it as a check on private power as necessary in a functioning democracy.

Our Gilded Age and Where It May Lead

Once upon a time, the major industrialized nations might have been thought to have learned their lesson. After suffering communist and fascist revolutions, a depression and two catastrophic World Wars, they had collectively changed their approach to the economy and its role in a democracy. Rejecting *laissez faire*'s rule by the wealthy, communism's dictatorship of the proletariat, and fascism's state-directed economy, the West took a different path—the re-democratization of economic policy and a politics of wealth redistribution. That path yielded decades of economic growth that built middle classes, and saw a level of prosperity previously unknown to human history, reducing what had become a massive gap between rich and poor. As such, the economic achievements of Western democracies stole the thunder of both communism and fascism, whose calls for revolution were always driven by the unfairness and cruelty of unfettered capitalism.

No one economic policy overcame the inequalities produced by the Industrial Revolution and the consolidations of late twentieth century. But antitrust laws formed part of the story, meant to break the economic and political power of self-enriching trusts, and to resist the accumulation of wealth in monopoly and concentrated cartels. That was a mission reinforced by the

20   horrible lessons of fascist Germany and Japan, and their close partnerships between government and its main monopolies. One way or another, concentration and inequality had its effects. By the late 1960s, the share of national income going to the top 1 percent of earners had fallen to 8 percent, a far cry from the extreme inequality of the 1910s and 1920s. Seemingly, the capitalist nations had found a way to square the circle, and by promising a wealthy middle class, presented an alluring alternative to the self-enriching dictatorships in other parts of the world.

That was then, and yet here we are again, as if trapped in a bad movie sequel. Today, as in the 1910s, two essential economic facts characterize the industrialized world. The first is the reemergence of an outrageous divide between the rich and the poor. This trend is most stark in the United States, where the top 1 percent today earn 23.8 percent of the national income and control an astonishing 38.6 percent of national wealth.

The second is a return to concentrated economies—that is, industries dominated by fewer and larger companies.* As the World Economic Forum attests, a smaller number of firms and industries control a far greater share of global wealth. In the

---

*There is a technical difference between "bigness" and "industry concentration"—the former refers just the size of firms, while the latter refers to the number of firms competing in each properly defined market. However, in practice, the two tend to overlap: When firms are larger in an industry, especially as a result of mergers, there tend to be fewer competing firms in the industry.

United States, between 1997 and 2012, 75 percent of American
industries became more concentrated. Similarly, since the year
2000, across U.S. industries, the Herfindahl-Hirschman index,
which measures market concentration, has increased in over 75
percent of industries. The stock markets have actually shrunk,
as the U.S. public markets have lost almost 50 percent of their
publicly traded firms.*

The most visible manifestations of the consolidation trend
sit right in front of our faces: the centralization of the once open
and competitive tech industries into just a handful of giants:
Facebook, Amazon, Google, and Apple. The power that these
companies wield seems to capture the sense of concern we
have that the problems we face transcend the narrowly economic. Big tech is ubiquitous, seems to know too much about
us, and seems to have too much power over what we see, hear,
do, and even feel. It has reignited debates over who really rules,
when the decisions of just a few people have great influence
over everyone. Their power feels like "a kingly prerogative,

*If industry concentration and income inequality are key features of our
economic times, are they linked? Many economists think so. See Jonathan
B. Baker & Steven C. Salop, *Antitrust, Competition Policy, and Inequality*,
104 Geo. L.J. Online 1 (2015). But the proposition is not uncontested. See
Daniel Crane, *Antitrust and Wealth Inequality*, 101 Cornell Law Review 1171
(2016). A concentrated industry can tacitly collude to prevent wage growth,
yielding less for workers and more for shareholders and management, and
be less competitive and more profitable, thanks to the ability to cooperate to
keep prices high or jointly exclude entrants. The profits are kept by profes-
sionals, senior executives, management, or shareholders, who are wealthier.
Concentrated industries can also cooperate politically to prevent redistribution or use government to protect profits.

22   inconsistent with our form of government" in the words of Senator John Sherman, for whom the Sherman Act is named.

With an economy that looks like a knock-off of the Guilded
Age, is it any surprise that our politics have come to match it?
The late nineteenth and early twentieth centuries were marked
by the brutal treatment of workers, the destruction of small-
and medium-sized businesses, and broad economic suffering.
That led to widespread popular anger and demands for something new and different. Strong leaders promised a return to
greatness, bread for the workers, and a new order.

Today, economic grievance is yielding a similar turn to
angry, populist answers around the world. Some blame their
fortunes on immigrants, Jews, Muslims, Christians, or perhaps the Chinese or the Americans, yielding a new generation
of xenophobic, nationalist, and racist politics. Others blame
bankers, the tech industry, or corporations in general. We have
witnessed a return to the politics of outrage and of violence, one
stoked by the humiliations of becoming poorer than one's parents, of workers who are treated as disposable, and the prospect
of falling through the cracks.

The better lesson from the twentieth century is that less
angry alternatives work: programs to aid the unemployed and
the aged, to protect workers and labor, and other efforts to blunt
the harshness and disparity inherent to unrestrained capitalism. And in the United States, there was born a different
movement and a different approach to tackling the structural
origins of accumulated private power, named after its target, the
trusts—hence the "antitrust" laws.

It would be an exaggeration to suggest that antitrust provides a full answer to either inequality or other economic

woes. But it does strike at the root cause of private political power—the economic concentration that facilitates political action. Advocating antitrust revival is not meant to compete with other economic proposals to address inequality. But laws that would redistribute wealth are themselves blocked by the enhanced political power of concentrated industries. In this way, the structure of the economy has an underlying influence on everything in the realm of economic policy. If antitrust is not the solution, it, historically, has been part of the solution, meriting a new look at what it can do.

To understand where we are and where we may be going, we must return to a moment in the past when we first began addressing the questions we still face today.

The Monopolization Movement

From the late nineteenth through the early twentieth century, the United States came under the grip of a powerful political and economic movement whose influence spread across the world and persists today. Known in its time as the Trust Movement, it called for the reorganization of the American and world economy into a new form: the giant, monopoly corporation. It achieved that goal with leviathans like Standard Oil and AT&T in America, I.G. Farben in Germany, and with the domination of the Japanese imperial economy by the *zaibatsu* system. In its American form, the Trust Movement envisioned an economy with every sector run by a single, almighty monopoly, fashioned out of hundreds of smaller firms, unfettered by competitors or government restraint. In short: pure economic autocracy.

This monopolization movement proceeded with blinding speed in the United States. During just one decade, from 1895 to 1904, at least 2,274 manufacturing firms merged, leaving behind 157 corporations, most of which dominated their indus-tries.* By the early 1900s, nearly every major industry in the United States was either already controlled by, or coming under the control of, a single monopolist. John D. Rockefeller's Stan-dard Oil remains the best-known monopoly of the era, but the greater economic impact came from the consolidation cam-paigns waged by men like banker John Pierpont Morgan, his-tory's greatest monopolizer. Morgan merged hundreds of steel firms into U.S. Steel, built railroad monopolies in the West and the Northeast, created an Atlantic shipping giant called the International Mercantile Marine Co., and served as the real force behind AT&T's conquest of the telecommunications industry. His model also inspired other copycat financiers who created a tobacco trust, a cotton trust, a sugar trust, a rubber trust, a film-makers trust, a trust that made matches, a nail trust, and so on.

To mention Morgan is to summon to mind the top hat, bulbous nose, giant yacht, and access to nearly unlimited cap-ital. His was called the Gilded Age for a reason, for the creation of industry-spanning monopolies was the source of a new kind of wealth that left bankers like Morgan or magnates like Rockefeller with personal fortunes and economic influence previously unknown to the world. To take just one example: To create the U.S. Steel monopoly, and eliminate Andrew Carnegie as a competitor, Morgan agreed to pay him a sum that

---

*Economic historian Naomi Lamoreaux traced the market shares of ninety-three of the major consolidations during that era, and recognized that seventy-two of them were able to gain at least a 40 percent market share in their industry, and forty-two of them gained over 70 percent. *The Great Merger Movement in American Business*, 1895–1904 (1985).

26   immediately made Carnegie the richest man in the world, and one of the richest in history. (Carnegie would soon thereafter be worth about $310 billion in current dollars measured by his share of the economy.) But even if the cash payouts of the Trust Movement provided much of the gusto, there was more to it than that. The new monopolists of the Gilded Age preferred to believe that they were not merely profiteering, but building a new and better society. They were bravely constructing a new order that discarded old ways and replaced them with an enlightened future characterized by rule by the strong, by a new kind of industrial Übermensch who transcended humanity's limitations. The new monopolies were the natural successor to competition, just as man had evolved from the ape.

The Trust Movement's arguments were, in part, economic: Men like Rockefeller and Morgan simply took the monopoly as a superior form of business organization that was saving the economy from ruin. The U.S. and world economy had undergone terrible shocks in the 1890s, and hundreds of firms were thrown into bankruptcy. Many blamed "ruinous competition" for driving prices too low. In the same way that Silicon Valley's Peter Thiel today argues that monopoly "drives progress" and that "competition is for losers," adherents to the Trust Movement thought Adam Smith's fierce competition had no place in a modern, industrialized economy.

Monopolists liked to portray themselves as part of a progressive movement, striving toward a better age, and justified their work using the then-fashionable ideology of "Social Darwinism" and the writings of its English exponent, Herbert Spencer. Not well known in our times, except, perhaps, as

crudely reflected in the writings of novelist Ayn Rand or the
monopoly worship of Thiel and other Silicon Valley thinkers,
Spencer provided a philosophy for the conquering tycoon, and,
for some, even a personal religion.

Here was the faith. Led by the strongest and greatest of
men, society was in the midst of an evolutionary transforma-
tion, whose goal was nothing less than the forging of a new
world order. The weak, the small, and the old-fashioned were
all being swept away, to be replaced by the new, the scientific,
and above all, the strong. For some, this purge displaced not just
old ways and inefficient businesses, but Christianity as well,
with its regard for the disadvantaged and insistence on humility
before God. Many Social Darwinists believed less in humanity's sinful nature than man's perfectibility, personified in the
image of a man "looking to the sun," aspiring to Godlike quali-
ties. The meek were not going to inherit the earth but be eliminated, through the process of a survival of the fittest.

In politics, Social Darwinists embraced *laissez-faire*, op-
posing any interventions that might be thought to stop the
strong from displacing the weak. Spencer opposed "poor laws"
in Britain, believing the impoverished should be left to live or
die on their own, so as "to clear the world of them, and make
room for better." To be fair, he and other Social Darwinists
did lend support in one form of state intervention: eugenics
campaigns meant to cull the physically and mentally disabled,
and thereby help speed up the coming of the new age. John
D. Rockefeller, Jr., would personally fund an initiative to
sterilize some 15 million Americans, for, as Spencer put it,
"The forces which are working out the great scheme of perfect

28 happiness. . . exterminate such sections of mankind as stand in their way, with the same sternness that they exterminate beasts of prey and herds of useless ruminants."

As between men, so would it be for business. Nothing—certainly not government—should try to stop the great monopolists in their conquest of the economy. For what was underway was a kind of industrial eugenics campaign that exterminated the weak and the unfit to make room for firms great and powerful. John D. Rockefeller, Jr. put it this way: "The American Beauty Rose can be produced in its splendor and fragrance only by sacrificing the early buds which grow up around it."

Resistance, such as would be waged by Louis Brandeis and his like, was futile, for Morgan's and Rockefeller's campaigns were thought to be natural, unstoppable, and perhaps even ordained by God. "To stop co-operation of individuals and aggregation of capital would be to arrest the wheels of progress—to stay the march of civilization—to decree immobility of intellect and degradation of humanity," explained Standard Oil's counsel Samuel Dodd, inventor of the Trust form. "You might as well endeavor to stay the formation of the clouds, the falling of the rains, or the flowing of the streams." Or, as Rockefeller himself put it, "Growth of a large business is merely a survival of the fittest . . . the working out of a law of nature, and a law of God."

This was the Trust Movement's underlying philosophy and vision of what an economy should be: centralized, run by great men, free from any government interference, and to promote survival of the fittest, largely indifferent to the plight or demise of the weak, the poor, and the unfit. It cannot be

denied that some of the firms built during this era were
impressive creations, and that the American economy, as a
whole, experienced impressive if not wholly unprecedented
growth. But the monopolization movement also marked a
radical break from values once seen as foundational to the
Republic, if not the more humanist traditions of Western civilization. As historian Richard Hofstadter put it, "Nothing less
was at stake that the entire organization of American business
and American politics, the very question of who was to control
the country."

For the American tradition had, to that point, been defined
by resistance to centralized power and monopoly. The American Revolution itself was in large part sparked by the abuses of
Crown monopolies. The original Boston Tea Party was, after all,
really an anti-monopoly protest. As Hofstadter writes: "From
its colonial beginnings through most of the nineteenth century, [America] was overwhelmingly a nation of farmers and
small-town entrepreneurs—ambitious, mobile, optimistic,
speculative, anti-authoritarian, egalitarian, and competitive.
As time went on, Americans came to take it for granted that
property would be widely diffused, that economic and political
power would be decentralized."

With the assertion that much of economic decision-
making was beyond the government's control, the question of
who really ruled the country was suddenly unclear. Fortifying
matters was the tendencies of great monopolists, like Standard Oil or the New Haven Railroad, to use bribes and other
forms of influence to control political outcomes. As such, the
movement posed a new challenge for a Constitution that was

30   committed to limited and separate powers, and never contemplated the rise of private power as great as any of the branches of government, and able to corrupt governmental operations to suit its ends.

Perhaps most profound was the break with the ideal that the United States was a nation characterized by a relative sense of equality among its citizens. As Alexis De Tocqueville observed, "Among the novel objects that attracted my attention during my stay in the United States, nothing struck me more forcibly than the general equality of condition among the people." But that was no longer true for small businesses, farmers, and especially workers. There was a new divide between the giant corporation and its workers, leading to strikes, violence, and a constant threat of class warfare. Looking back, the difference in incomes was so stark it makes today's America look like Scandinavia; the wealthy might earn millions a year, while the average worker earned between one and two dollars a day.

In short, while the Trust Movement was powerful, lucrative, and had its true believers, it also engendered great popular resistance that threatened a new revolution. Overseas, socialist, communist, and anarchist forces were gaining strength and would in time overthrow many of Europe's governments. In the United States, outrage was channeled into organized labor, the farmers' "Granger movement," the founding of an Anti-Monopoly Party, and the emergence of populist candidates like William Jennings Bryan, three-time Democratic nominee for President.

And it also led to the passage of the first antitrust law, the Sherman Act, enacted in 1890, during the first furious wave of reactions to the rise of the trusts. The law was named after its original sponsor, Senator John Sherman, an Ohio Republican who was the younger brother of the Civil War general William Tecumseh Sherman. While it was clear that the law was meant to address the "Trust Problem," like many laws, the reasons stated for its passage were many and varied, reflecting a then-recent debate over tariff policy, as well as the interests of small producers, farmers, and others, as modified by the usual dealmaking and compromises. The language of the law is extremely broad. In section one it bans "every contract, combination in the form of trust or otherwise . . . in restraint of trade." In section two it declares that "every person who shall monopolize, or attempt to monopolize . . . any part of the trade or commerce among the several States, or with foreign nations, shall be deemed guilty of a felony."

The language is so strong—its literal text bans so much—that the scholarly debate over the Sherman Act's meaning and history may never end. But two things can be stated. It was clearly understood as a reaction to the rising power of the monopoly trusts, such as the Standard Oil company. And it was evident that the members of Congress had concerns that were diverse and disparate in nature. Consider, for example, the words of Senator Sherman on the floor of the Senate, who discussed the evils of monopoly pricing, but also proclaimed that no problem "is more threatening than the inequality of condition, of wealth, and opportunity" and also added that "if the concerted powers of this combination are entrusted to a single man, it is a kingly prerogative, inconsistent with our form of government."

32   Let us not spend any more time on the impossible task of trying to find the true original meaning of the Sherman Act. Instead, we turn to the work of Louis Brandeis, whose philosophy of resistance to the Trust Movement and whose vision of the economy has had an enduring influence, and whose voice is needed for what we confront today.

The Right to Live, and Not Merely to Exist

Louis Brandeis, the advocate, reformer, and Supreme Court Justice, has been done a particular kind of disservice. He is still known as a great jurist; his writings on the First Amendment and privacy are exalted. But what Brandeis really cared about was the economic conditions under which life is lived, and the effects of the economy on one's character and on the nation's soul.

This book aspires to resurrect and try to renovate the lost tenets of the Brandeisian economic vision. It envisions a vigorous, healthy economy, a skepticism of the self-serving rhetoric projecting the romance of big business or the inevitability of monopoly, and, above all, a sensitivity to human ends. Brandeis took matters like bigness and concentration as inseparable from the very nature of democracy, and the conditions under which its citizens would live. They determined what kind of country we would live in and what kind of environment that country would provide for its citizens.

Louis Brandeis was born in 1856, in the mid-sized town of Louisville, Kentucky, the son of entrepreneurial immigrants. As is probably true of most of us but is easier to see in Brandeis, these early years would have an important influence over what he thought an economy should ideally look like in a democracy.

His father, Adolph, was born in Prague, to a middle-class family. Adolph decided to take his chances in the Midwest at what was then the American frontier. He was not a particularly good farmer, but found greater success as a grain merchant in Kentucky, and grew to be a prosperous small-business owner. Brandeis's mother Frederika, the daughter of a Polish court physician, was a devotee of eighteenth-century German authors like Friedrich Schiller and Johann Wolfgang von Goethe, and a moralist who pushed her children to develop "a pure spirit and the highest ideals as to morals and love."

The town of Louisville would figure essentially in what Brandeis would come to stand for. Louisville was no world capital, nor the seat of any corporate empire, but nonetheless a flourishing regional center, in a United States far more economically decentralized than today's. It was, economically speaking, dominated by no few large concerns but a multitude of small producers. While the state still suffered the curse of agricultural slavery, Louisville was, at least to Brandeis, an "idyllic" place, one free from the "curse of bigness," representing an "economic democracy"—that is, a place of industrial freedom and openness to competition, yet with an economy that yielded adequate spoils for all. "Louisville [during his youth]" writes Brandeis biographer Melvin

Urofsky, "seemed the quintessential democratic society, in which individuals, like his father and Mr. Crawford, could do well by dint of their intelligence and perseverance. There were no large factories employing thousands of people, but rather many small endeavors—farms, stores, professional offices. People knew one another, their lives entwined in a strong sense of community."

After high school, Brandeis studied in Germany, achieved famously high grades at Harvard Law School, and developed a passion for canoeing and horseback riding. He decided to make his career in Boston, built a distinguished legal practice, and might have otherwise lived a completely uneventful life had he not been stirred into politics and action by his outrage to that which was happening around him. For in the 1890s, by the time he reached his forties, the Trust movement had begun its full march on the American economy, acquiring and demolishing smaller businesses and independents right and left. Many of Brandeis's clients were small-business owners with whom he had a personal relationship. They became the targets of the economic eugenics movement, seen as too unfit to deserve industrial life. In his resistance to the Trust movement, which at times he seemed to compare to a pogrom, Brandeis gained his identity and formulated the principles of economic decentralization that are now his legacy.

Brandeis's views crystalized during a battle with a tributary of the Morgan empire. Among Morgan's many projects was the consolidation of the Northeastern rail and ferry transportation into one monopoly—the New Haven Railroad. Morgan and his anointed lieutenant, Charles Mellen, sought

36   to combine some 336 firms, including Boston's local rail-road, the Boston and Maine, to forge a new system. Brandeis would become the monopolization campaign's leading public opponent.

Brandeis, who was a business lawyer by trade, and did insurance work in his earlier years, was hardly unsympathetic to the role business played in society. He was happy to praise good businesses that grew organically and built dignified operations beloved by customers and partners—the model provided by his own father. But during his fight with Morgan and the New Haven railroad, he developed a distrust, even a disgust with the new class of corporate monopoly. For behind the happy talk and big promises, his own investigations suggested that the New Haven was building its monopoly by lying to investors, bribing politicians, and paying off journalists and professors. "Lying and sneaking are always bad, no matter what the ends" said Brandeis later, privately. "I don't care about punishing crime, but I am implacable in maintaining standards."

Over time, he came to believe the New Haven represented the evils of what he called "excessive bigness." As he put it, "the evils of excessive bigness are something distinct from and additional to the evils of monopoly. A business may be too big to be efficient without being a monopoly; and it may be a monopoly and yet (so far as concerns size) may be well within the limits of efficiency. Unfortunately, the so-called New Haven system suffers from both excessive bigness and from monopoly."

But Brandeis's opposition to the New Haven monopolization campaign was, at first, a failure. He was just one man against Morgan and his resources—and Mellen, a charismatic charmer, who won over the press and locals by promising New England "progress and prosperity." As for Brandeis, Mellen discounted him this way: "Yellow dogs will bark and snap at the wheels of progress as they have since the beginning of time. Men will come and go, but the system of transportation has been built up to endure." But Brandeis knew the New Haven had, in fact, been built on a house of cards. As with many mega-mergers, organizational chaos soon followed the consolidation. Morgan's aggressive firing of workers and other cost-cutting measures were necessary to generate returns promised to shareholders, but they led to wrecks, derailments, and delays. There were 24 deaths and 105 injuries in 1911 alone. As the railroad fell into decline, the press began to turn on the New Haven and Morgan. One newspaper owner wrote: "Mr. Morgan holds the gun of monopoly at the head of business, and business, as a rule, prefers to give up its money and preserve its life."

The chaos prompted new investigations, and in 1913 the Federal Interstate Commerce Commission unearthed evidence of serious accounting fraud and illicit payouts in the monopolization drive. As the Commission wrote, the consolidation campaign had "meant the reckless and scandalous expenditure of money; it meant the attempt to control public opinion; corruption of government; the attempt to pervert the political and economic instincts of the people in insolent defiance of law." The Justice Department threatened an antitrust lawsuit in 1914 and the New Haven was broke, dissolved back into its major pieces.

Through the New Haven experience, Brandeis discovered a stronger faith in decentralized systems, in the organic growth

38   of business, and, for want of a better word, in "smallness."
He prized, indeed lionized, the human scale that had been
the trademark of business and farming in America. Despite the
bold promises of men like Mellen and Morgan, Brandeis feared
that the new trusts being crafted by combining entire industries were not really the progress that was promised. Instead, he
watched them exterminate other businesses, mistreat workers,
defraud investors, and, especially in the case of the New Haven,
actually hide gross inefficiencies with their size—all in the service of profits for bankers and speculators. He feared that as the
corporations became large and powerful, they took on a life of
their own, becoming increasingly insensitive to humanity's
wants and fears. He put it this way in 1911: "We are in a position, after the experience of the last twenty years, to state two
things: In the first place, that a corporation may well be too large
to be the most efficient instrument of production and of distribution, and, in the second place, whether it has exceeded the
point of greatest economic efficiency or not, it may be too large
to be tolerated among the people who desire to be free."

If pre-industrial Louisville represented Brandeis's idea of
what a democracy and economy might look like structurally, we
can also gain from his later writings some idea of what Brandeis
thought a democratic economy was *for*. Nowadays, we may
think that the economy serves to make us rich, or at least to pay
the bills. Democracy, meanwhile, is about voting for a government that reflects our preferences.

Brandeis demanded more from the economy and democracy. For him, the very purpose of life was the building of good
character and the development of self. The "ideal" of democracy,

he once said, should be "the development of the individual for his own and the common good." He was in accord with the position taken by contemporary philosopher Wilhelm Von Humboldt, who wrote that "the true end of man, or that which is prescribed by the eternal or immutable dictates of reason . . . is the highest and most harmonious development of his powers to a complete and consistent whole."*

That view had important implications for what the nation and its laws should look like. A worthy nation was one that served as cauldron for character and self-development, one that "compels us to strive for the development of the individual." Importantly, Brandeis didn't think that such personal growth was something that just happened: He believed that it required the right conditions. As he said: "The 'right to life' guaranteed by our Constitution" should be understood as "the right to live, and not merely to exist. In order to live men must have the opportunity of developing their faculties; and they must live under conditions in which their faculties may develop naturally and healthily."

A good country and a good economy, therefore, would be one that provided to everybody sufficient liberties and adequate

---

*His lofty ideals may make Brandeis sound like some kind of demigod walking the earth, but he was not without defects. The small businesses he praised were, after all, often his clients. And while warm and loving to his family members, he appears to have been a distant and aloof figure who had a way of making others feel inadequate in his presence, particularly in his later years. The jurist Learned Hand recalls his meetings with Brandeis this way: "I used to leave him [Brandeis] feeling [of myself], 'You are a self-indulgent, inadequate person.' . . . You sit around and talk a good deal, haven't any very definite convictions. You're not spending your life trying to leave the world better for being in it. You like to drink too much."

40   support to live meaningful, fulfilling lives. He thought the American founders had understood this, that "[t]hey valued liberty both as an end, and as a means. They believed liberty to be the secret of happiness, and courage to be the secret of liberty." Hence a worthy nation should protect men and women from any forces, public or private, that might stifle the opportunities for thriving and life. That would include, of course, government censorship and oppression—hence the importance of free speech, free association, and other liberties. But it also meant freedom from industrial domination, exploitation, or so much economic insecurity that one could not really live without fear of unemployment and poverty. "Men are not free," he wrote, "if dependent industrially on the arbitrary will of another." Economic security was a foundation on which one could really be free in a meaningful sense—hence the importance of steady but not oppressive work, of education, time and space for leisure, parks, libraries, and other institutions.

What Brandeis noticed is something we often ignore. We like to speak of freedoms in the abstract, but for most people, a sense of autonomy is more influenced by private forces and economic structure than by government. For many if not most people, the conditions of work determine how much of life is lived—such basic matters as the length of hours worked, the threat of being fired, harassment or mistreatment by a boss, and for some jobs, questions as fundamental as personal safety or access to a bathroom. Beyond work, our daily lives are shaped profoundly by economic matters like rent, access to transportation or groceries, and health insurance, even more so than any abstract freedoms. That is why Brandeis saw real freedom as freedom from both public *and* private coercion.*

Brandeis saw an economy dominated by giant corporations as tending to a certain inhumanity. He feared that working in a giant corporation might rob the American people of their character: "far more serious than even the suppression of competition is the suppression of industrial liberty, indeed of manhood itself." He grew to detest the growing American culture of overwork, whether self-inflicted, as in the private lawyer's case, or more menacingly, in the growing class of large firms who worked their employees past the limits of human endurance. As he once wrote of the oppressive conditions and long hours at the new industrial firms, they threatened to create "a life so inhuman as to make our former Negro slavery infinitely preferable."

Instead what Brandeis really believed was that business could be a high calling and that a good career was one that created the conditions for human thriving. He thought for most people, a truly successful career consisted in developing a skill or a craft, or building a good business, and practicing as best one could, while aspiring to live by high principles in both personal and business affairs. That was the path to career happiness, yet was too often forgotten by those trying to gain an advantage or making the grave error of taking income or wealth as the measure of success. "A large income is the ordinary incident of

---

*An insensitivity to private intrusions on human freedom is a major blind spot for contemporary libertarianism, which is rightly concerned with government overreach but bizarrely tolerant of mistreatment or abuse committed by so-called private actors.

42   success" he wrote "but he who exaggerates the value of the incident is apt to fail of real success." Instead, the honorable pro-
fessions "select as their test, excellence of performance in the
broadest sense—and include, among other things, advance in
the particular occupation and service to the community. . . ."

How did Brandeis's principles manifest themselves more
broadly, as economic policy? Brandeis took the view that government's highest role lay in the protection of human liberty
and the provision of securities consistent with human thriving.
That meant a commitment to civil liberties, like rights of free
speech and privacy, protected by the courts. But it also meant a
commitment to the protection of workers, and an open economy
composed of smaller firms—along with measures to break or
limit the power of monopolies.

Hence, if the antitrust laws might decentralize the economy, so much the better. If other laws might do the same, that
was good, too. Beyond that, Brandeis thought there should be
no business exception for ethics, but that government should
punish those who used abusive, oppressive, or unconscio-
nable business methods to succeed. That's why some of his
greatest ire was reserved for abusive consolidation campaigns
that offended both his sense of ethics and economics, where
businesses were forced into sales to avoid being bankrupted or
destroyed by a powerful rival.

On the positive side Brandeis was an advocate of measures
designed to make life worth living, or foster a republic of good
character and true citizenry. That meant good public education,
steady but not outrageous work hours, pensions for the aged,

and sufficient time for leisure and study. He wanted child labor   43
to be banned, and the imposition of maximum work hours for
others. In short, he wanted the nation to be a place with room
for citizens to thrive, not merely to survive.

We have now some general, though incomplete idea of
Brandeis' life and ideals.* Politically, he does not easily fit into
contemporary categories. He worked as an advocate for business
and business groups, yet also supported unions in their struggle
with large employees, and believed that workers should fight
for constant work and their fair share of the economic returns.
He distrusted big government almost as much as big business,
especially at the federal level, but felt that antitrust laws needed
to be vigorously enforced. If he had a unifying principle, politically and economically, it is what we have said: that concentrated power in any form is dangerous, that institutions should
be built to human scale, and society should pursue human ends.
Every institution, public and private, runs the risks of taking
on a life of its own, putting its own interests above those of the
humans it was supposedly created to serve.

*Brandeis is not without his critics. Historian Thomas McCraw took his best
shot at Brandeis in his book *Prophets of Regulation* (1984), portraying him as
too rigid and unwilling to accept the potential for efficiency and consumer
benefits in new, giant businesses being built. Unfortunately, McCraw makes
several basic errors in his attack, like confusing horizontal price-fixing with
retail price maintenance. And McCraw seems to have misunderstood the
role of a public advocate: Brandeis was fighting against a well-funded campaign to transform the American economy based on what he believed to be
a false narrative of progress. What McCraw calls rigidity can also be called
principle; what has sustained interest in Brandeis for so long is his adher-
ence to ideals in a manner that transcended day-to-day politics, without
being so removed as to be irrelevant.

44   Brandeis's importance lies in his lasting vision of what an economy should be for. But while he fought the good fight, particularly against large mergers, the credit for actually activating the antitrust laws belongs elsewhere. In particular, it belongs to the man who would soon use the antitrust laws as his big stick.

The Trustbuster

There are many ways that the history of both the United States and the world might have been different had not a strange man named Leon Czolgosz, using a pistol concealed by a handkerchief, shot President William McKinley twice in the abdomen on September 6, 1901, while shaking his hand at the Temple of Music in Buffalo. This much is certain: American economic history changed decisively in that moment.

Under President McKinley, *laissez-faire* was the unannounced, but nonetheless evident, economic policy of the United States. As biographer Edmund Morris puts it, McKinley "tacitly acknowledged that Wall Street, rather than the White House, had executive control of the economy. . . . This conservative alliance, forged after the Civil War, was intended to last well into the new century, if not forever." The doctrine of *laissez-faire,* a cousin to Social Darwinism, suggested that economic problems would tend to work themselves out, and hence government intervention would usually do more harm than good. Its American translation was, "Let well enough alone!"

46   That was the faith, and as such it took on Constitutional dimen-
      sions. For it dictated that not even Congress or elected repre-
      sentatives were to "interfere" with the economy; the economy
      had its own sovereignty. Laws seeking to ban child labor, or set
      maximum work hours were, by this thinking, unconstitutional
      intrusions into the economy's natural operation.*

      McKinley's *laissez-faire* views had left the Sherman Act,
      then a newly enacted antitrust law, in a stillbirth from which
      it was not clear it would ever emerge. Men like McKinley took
      the law as merely symbolic, a resolution meant to appease the
      populist wings of both parties. Others thought it simply reaf-
      firmed pre-existing practices of the courts, and hence did not
      change anything. McKinley's main concession to growing
      public arousal and unrest in the late 1890s was to discuss the
      "Trust problem" in one State of the Union speech, and suggest
      it was something Congress really ought to deal with some day. It
      was as if the Sherman Act did not exist.

      That impression was only confirmed, in 1901, when it be-
      came known that J. P. Morgan was now planning to buy out
      Andrew Carnegie and create the U.S. Steel trust. While it was
      a flagrant violation of the Sherman Act, the McKinley White
      House offered no public comment and instead held a dinner in
      Morgan's honor.

      But now President McKinley lay dying, suffering from
      gangrene, after surgeons failed to locate the bullet lodged in
      his body. A firsthand report of Morgan's reaction to the news

      *In subsequent years, the courts would strike down such laws as unconsti-
      tutional, in cases like *Lochner v. New York*, 198 U.S. 45 (1905) (striking down
      a law setting maximum work hours) and *Hammer v. Dagenhart*, 247 U.S. 251
      (1918) (holding a ban on child labor unconstitutional).

of McKinley's shooting has him seizing the arm of the reporter
from the *New York Times*: "What?" and then slumping into a desk
chair, exclaiming: "This is sad, sad, very sad news." Upon his
death, Senator Mark Hanna, one of McKinley's closest friends
and conservative allies, publicly declaimed, "Now look—that
damned cowboy is President of the United States!" And Morgan
was right to be concerned, for the death of McKinley did change
everything, putting economic policy in the hands of an entirely
different kind of man.

Theodore Roosevelt may not need a full introduction. He was
born to a wealthy family, but was a man whose democratic lean-
ings were unmistakable. In his storied career, in his rise from New
York City police commissioner to Assistant Secretary of the Navy
to the Presidency, he managed to combine an imperial tempera-
ment with an ear for public sentiment. He was not anti-business,
but strongly insistent on punishing villainy when he saw it, and
most of all he believed that a majoritarian government must
lead the country. His determination that the public was ruler
over the corporation, and not vice versa, would make him the
single most important advocate of a political antitrust law.

Roosevelt's revolt and rejection of *laissez-faire* was actually
evident two weeks before McKinley's assassination. He gave a
landmark speech in Minnesota asserting that it was time for the
State to assert its authority over the trusts. "The vast individual
and corporate fortunes, the vast combinations of capital which
have marked the development of our industrial system," he said,
"create new conditions, and necessitate a change from the old
attitude of the State and the nation toward property."

But Roosevelt's legacy lies not merely in his rhetoric. A law
like the Sherman Act is, without enforcement, a dead letter.

48   That's why a focus on enforcement of the law is so critical to the story of the war against the trusts. And here Roosevelt was not a man to content to play around at the edges. As president, he would soon directly confront the two greatest monopolists of the age, who were the very backbone of the trust movement— J. P. Morgan, and then John D. Rockefeller—in what can only be described as acts of enormous courage.

His offensive against Morgan came first, and it was sparked by the latter's railroad monopolization. In 1901, at just about the time Roosevelt was taking the presidency, Morgan and another railroad magnate, James J. Hill, were effecting the monopolization of Western railroad transportation. Morgan forged a truce among former rivals (including Rockefeller), embodied in a new trust, the Northern Securities Company, representing a new, unified monopoly over all of the Western railroads, instantiated in a New Jersey Trust corporation. It was what is today called a "merger to monopoly" and clearly violated the Sherman Act.

Had he still been in power, President McKinley would almost certainly have "let well enough alone," as he had the U.S. Steel merger, or perhaps asked Morgan, in confidence, for a few concessions. But Roosevelt, in one of his first main actions as president, ordered his Attorney General Philander Knox to begin an investigation of the Northern Securities Company, and to review its legality under the Sherman Act. Knox, perhaps prodded by Roosevelt, stunned the political and financial world with an announcement: "In my judgment, [the Northern Securities Company] violates the provisions of the Sherman Act of 1890."

Why did Roosevelt order the investigation? Roosevelt was far less wary of size as a danger unto itself than a man like Brandeis. He held a real affection for the greatness and majesty of large institutions. Nor did he hold a personal animus toward Morgan himself—they were both of the New York aristocracy, and he'd personally invited Morgan to White House dinners.

For Roosevelt it was a matter of political democracy. He plainly saw the growing power of the trusts as a serious political question, as a threat to the basic proposition of democratic rule. To Roosevelt, economic policy did not form an exception to popular rule, and he viewed the seizure of economic policy by Wall Street and trust management as a serious corruption of the democratic system. He also understood, as we should today, that ignoring economic misery and refusing to give the public what they wanted would drive a demand for more extreme solutions, like Marxist or anarchist revolution. Hence, as he later said, "When aggregated wealth demands what is unfair, its immense power can be met only by the still greater power of the people as a whole." And, as he wrote to a friend at the time, "the absolutely vital question" was whether "the government has the power to control the trusts."

A few weeks after Knox's determination, at the direction of Roosevelt and his cabinet, the United States filed suit against the Northern Securities Company, beginning the first great judicial attack, by the federal government, on a private trust and on the personal economic power of J. P. Morgan himself.

Later in life, Roosevelt would give his account of Morgan's reaction.* Soon after suit was filed, an indignant and angry Morgan arrived at the White House and demanded to see the

*We don't have Morgan's account of the meeting, and Roosevelt tended to tell stories in a manner so as to make himself look courageous, so the account given should be taken with a grain of salt.

50   president. He was granted an audience, where Morgan complained of the lack of notice, and proposed that their lawyers meet to settle the matter. "If we have done anything wrong," said Morgan, "send your man to my man and they can fix it up." But Roosevelt responded, "that can't be done," and Knox added, "we don't want to fix it up, we want to stop it." Morgan, quietly furious at the challenge to his power, demanded to know whether his prize creation, U.S. Steel, would also be coming under attack. "Certainly not," said Roosevelt, "unless we find out that in any case they've done something we regard as wrong." When Morgan had left, Roosevelt summarized the meeting this way: "Mr. Morgan could not help regarding me as a big rival operator who either intended to ruin all his interests or could be induced to come to an agreement."

It was at around this time that the word "trust-buster" (and its occasional synonym, "octopus hunter") came into widespread popular usage. It became Roosevelt's appellation; he became the trustbuster incarnate. It was the image inhabited by Roosevelt in print and editorial cartoons, given color by the President's bold declarations. Over the summer of 1902, during the campaign against Morgan, he gave a speech in Rhode Island where he announced that "a man of great wealth who does not use that wealth decently is, in a peculiar sense, a menace to the community." He added that the "trusts are the creatures of the State, and the State not only has the right to control them, but it is in duty bound to control them wherever need of such control is shown."

And so here begins the trust-busting tradition in its hour of greatest glory. Its significance cannot be overstated. A law like the Sherman Act, like the Constitution, is so broadly worded and unclear in its application that it does not take real meaning or

shape without an enforcement tradition. In the person of Roosevelt was born the archetype: the courageous government official
unafraid of the massive private power represented by the trusts,
the incorruptible sheriff of economic justice. As the *Washington
Star* put it, "The President of the United States is the original
'trust-buster,' the great and only one for this occasion."

In the century to follow, the trustbuster mantle would be
something like a magic cape, or perhaps suit of armor, embold-
ening its wearer, that would be passed down through the generations. It would be inhabited first by Taft, Roosevelt's successor,
who was even more aggressive that Roosevelt. It would be worn
by prominent Justice Department officials, including, among
others, Robert Jackson, who would also be a Nuremberg prose-
cutor, and by Supreme Court Justice Thurman Arnold, the Wyoming "cowboy" and Yale professor who became the New Deal's
most aggressive trustbuster. It also belonged to Joel Klein, who
in the 1990s faced off with Bill Gates.

Along with the mantle and the archetype came a tradition,
one that lasted at least to the 1990s, of bringing "battleship"
cases against giant, industry-spanning monopolists. These
declarations of war against giant firms were not for the faint of
heart. The cases could last years, if not decades, and demand
resources that strained even the richest government on Earth.
They also tended to yield political attacks and efforts to ruin
government agencies like the Justice Department and the Federal Trade Commission, not to mention personal attacks as
well.

The Northern Securities litigation itself went relatively
quickly: The Justice Department asserted that the establishment of the firm was an attempt to monopolize the railroad

52   business, in violation of Section 2 of the Sherman Act. The company's main defense was that the federal government had no authority to stop its mergers; it had no right to punish the mere transfer of property and establishment of a new state corporation. In the alternate, it responded that its goals were, in fact, entirely beneficent: It wished to enhance and extend commerce across the West, and benefit the public through a better railroad.

After two full trials (one contested by Minnesota), the case eventually made its way to the Supreme Court. In a major victory for Roosevelt, the antitrust law, and the Congress of 1890, the merger was blocked. The opinion was written by Justice John Marshall Harlan, a great antitrust absolutist, who spoke for the agrarian and populist spirit behind the Sherman Act's creation, and would become a leading judicial voice supporting the early trust-busting tradition.

Harlan read the Sherman Act as a literal ban on trusts, which, as he would later say, presented the danger of a "slavery that would result from aggregations of capital in the hands of a few individuals and corporations." With the *Northern Securities* opinion he effectively awoke the Sherman Act's anti-monopoly powers. For him, the western railroad trust was a blatant violation of the Sherman Act's prohibitions. For it "placed the control of the two roads in the hands of a single person, to wit, the Securities Company, . . . [and] destroy[ed] every motive for competition between two roads . . . by pooling the earnings of the two roads for the common benefit of the stockholders of both companies."

Despite Harlan's certainty, the decision was a close one, won on a 5–4 vote, and the famous dissenter, Justice Oliver Wendell Holmes, took the view that the Sherman Act was not,

in fact, meant to outlaw the trusts or even to protect competition. Instead, according to Holmes, "it was the ferocious
extreme of competition with others, not the cessation of competition among the partners, that was the evil feared." In other
words, Holmes held the bizarre idea that ruinous competition
was the concern of the Sherman Act, a theory hard to square
with its text or history.*

In the end, *Northern Securities* was an important victory for
Roosevelt and his premise that the trusts must obey the state,
for he had challenged and humbled a man, J. P. Morgan, who had
once seemed beyond the reach of any law, a man who nations
might obey rather than order. As Roosevelt later reflected, "it
was imperative to teach the masters of the biggest corporations
in the land that they were not, and would not be permitted to
regard themselves as, above the law."

Political Antitrust

When Roosevelt activated the Sherman Act, his goal was as
much political as economic. He saw enforcement of the Act
as essential to making clear that, in a democracy, the elected

---

*As a matter of legal method, Holmes's reading is hard to support, and his
opinion is in direct tension with his views, expressed in later opinions (like
his *Lochner* dissent) that favored the majority's right to decide economic
policy, no matter what the judiciary might think. Perhaps he thought that
the Sherman Act was only ever meant to be symbolic, the kind of strong
but unenforceable statement legislatures occasionally make to placate the
public. It is also the case that Holmes had himself become sympathetic to
the idea that the trusts were an evolutionary improvement over "wasteful"
competition. In a private letter he wrote that "there are great wastes in competition, due to advertisement, superfluous reduplication of establish-
ments, etc. But those are the very things the trusts get rid of."

54   representatives ultimately had the final say, and saw the anti-
      trust laws as one antidote to danger of private economic power
      that might rival public power. As Justice William Douglas would
      later put it, "power that controls the economy should be in the
      hands of elected representatives of the people, not in the hands
      of an industrial oligarchy." Hence the idea that antitrust would
      play a Constitutional role.

      But what does it mean to say that antitrust plays a "Con-
      stitutional" role? As every American schoolchild knows, the
      U.S. Constitution is comprised of a system of checks and bal-
      ances. The legislature is supposed to check executive power,
      and vice versa; the judiciary provides checks on the legislature,
      the executives, and the states as well. Hence, antitrust law was
      serving as a new kind of limit: a check on *private* power, by pre-
      venting the growth of monopoly corporations into something
      that might transcend the power of elected government to con-
      trol. His pursuit of this goal makes it fair to call Roosevelt the
      pioneer of political antitrust.

      In our times, when concerns about corporate influence over
      government have reached a fever pitch, the political impor-
      tance of antitrust as a check on private power might seem more
      obvious than ever. Yet over the last few decades, the very idea
      of political role has all but disappeared, as antitrust's focus has
      become exclusively and narrowly economic. It isn't as if the laws
      have been amended: The legislatures repeatedly expressed fear
      and concern with the accumulation of private power in compe-
      tition with government. As recently as 1962, the Supreme Court
      pointed out that the antitrust laws respond to a "concentration
      of economic power" and also a "threat to other values," like the
      independence of smaller businesses or local control of industry.

The retreat, rather, is best attributed to a combination of fear and uncertainty among those who enforce and interpret the laws—especially departments of government and federal judges. Political values, the argument goes, are just, well, too political or too vague to be considered part of enforcement policy.

This is not a good excuse. No one denies that economic considerations are what should govern any individual case. But the broad tenor of antitrust enforcement—the broader goals of enforcement—should be animated by a concern that too much concentrated economic power will translate into too much political power, and thereby threaten the Constitutional structure. Or, as Robert Pitofsky put it, we should always be concerned that "excessive concentration of economic power will breed antidemocratic political pressures."

Let's make plain what both Roosevelt and Pitofsky noticed: The compatibility of extreme industrial concentration and democratic government is an uncertain proposition. At some level the point is obvious: Private economic power is a rival to the power of elected governments, and firms may also seek to control politics for their own purposes. Increased industrial concentration predictably yields increased influence over political outcomes for corporations and business interests, as opposed to citizens or the public. But let us take a moment to see how political scientists have developed this point.

In a representative democracy, lawmaking is supposed to roughly match what the majority wants. If that is unclear or disputed, then we might expect or hope they'd reflect the interests of the "swing" voter—that is, the middle-of-the-road man or woman. But research shows that, for the vast majority of policy matters, that isn't how things work at all.

56   It was a scholar named Mancur Olson at Harvard who, in the 1960s, upended the understanding of political influence by pointing out that, in fact, large majorities don't get what they want on many issues. Instead, they consistently lose out to small, closely-knit groups with discrete interests around which they organize—of which the "industry association" is the best example. A group like "the middle class" or "consumers," while impressive in numbers and even theoretical economic power, faces major disadvantages in the actual political process. That follows because political influence—lobbying—requires organization, financial resources, time, and yields rewards that are not limited to those who put in the effort. Olson's memorable conclusion is that the small and organized will dominate the large and disorganized.

There are always a few inspired members of the public who devote their lives to political change. But their numbers pale in comparison to the paid ranks of corporate lobbyists, working at industry organizations, whose incentive is not altruism but generous salaries for achieving payouts through lawmaking. If one simply regards lobbying as an investment in political outcomes, the rewards are copious, and more than justify the money and effort. Consider, for example, the case of the pharmaceutical industry in the United States. In 2003, the industry invested $116 million in convincing Congress to ban America's largest federal-run insurance program, Medicare, from negotiating for lower drug prices. That $116 million was, to be sure, a major investment. However, the enactment of the negotiation ban has benefited the industry (and cost consumers) an estimated $90 billion per year. As an investment, it returns some

77,500 percent, and is a gift that keeps on giving. In recent years, when President Donald Trump, in a populist mood, proposed changing the law and forcing negotiations, the money began to flow, and lo and behold, the proposal went away.

Everyone knows that lobbying works. But a key and neglected point is that the relative consolidation of industry has an important influence on it. That follows because the fewer members of the industry, the fewer among whom the gains are split. Take the industry organization "Airlines for America." It has a limited number of members—three major airlines and seven smaller ones. The fruits of any policy success—say, preventing a cap on baggage and change fees—are immediately shared among the members.

Concentrated industries have good reasons to invest political influence. Consider, by contrast, the problem of collective action that faces "the middle class," a large group with some 100 million members. A middle-class tax cut might save each member $500 a year. However, it might also require someone to invest $50 million to lobby and ensure passage of that tax cut. As the math makes clear, there is no individual member of the middle class that has the incentive to make that investment. Even if it were just a $20 million lobbying price tag, there would still be no investment. This is the problem of collective action, and it predicts that large groups—the majority—will often be losers in the legislative process.

Advanced empirical research has begun to demonstrate that these predictions bear out. A Princeton and Northwestern group in 2014 tested various theories of politics and concluded that a theory of "biased pluralism" best explained outcomes—that the

58   public policies "tend to tilt toward the wishes of corporations and business and professional associations."

How does antitrust's approach to concentration relate to this? Simply enough: The more concentrated the industry, the fewer who need to coordinate, and the fewer among whom the stakes need be divided. If an industry has sixty or eighty firms in it, they may squabble, be incapable of acting as a group, and also face the problem of collective action. But, after consolidation, we might be speaking of just six firms, and the prospects for political cooperation improve. And after a merger to monopoly, there is no need to cooperate at all.

The simplest—if slightly overstated—way to put this is as follows. The more concentrated the industry, the more corrupted we can expect the political process to be. Here, by corrupted, we mean a political system that does not serve its stated goals—service of the public's interests—but instead favors a few groups at the expense of the general public.

All of this amounts to just a more fancy way of demonstrating Roosevelt's point: Concentrated private power can serve as a threat to the Constitutional design, and the enforcement of the antitrust law can provide a final check on private power. This, by itself, provides an independent rationale for enforcement of the antitrust laws.

The Abusive Trust

Roosevelt's confrontation with J. P. Morgan's western railroad monopoly in 1904 was neither timid nor trivial. But if blocking the formation of a new monopoly trust was one thing, what about all the trusts that were already running the economy? To put the question more bluntly, what about Standard Oil?

For there, unmolested, sat Standard Oil, the very first
trust. It held its monopoly for nearly twenty-five years. At the
time, it was the largest private firm in the world. Standard Oil's
patriarch, John D. Rockefeller, was in fact the wealthiest single
American in history, with an accumulated capital between $300
and $400 billion in today's dollars.

Quite a feat for a man born poor, to a father who was little
more than a confidence man. Once upon a time, in the late
1860s, "the Standard" had been just a mid-sized Cleveland
operation with no particular technological advantages over its
rivals. It did, however, have the strategic genius of Rockefeller
and his particular talent for industry conquest. As journalist
Ida Tarbell would write of him, Rockefeller "was like a general
who, besieging a city surrounded by fortified hills, views from
a balloon the whole great field, and see how, this point taken,
that must fall; this hill reached, that fort is commanded. And
nothing was too small: the corner grocery in Browntown, the
humble refining still on Oil Creek, the shortest private pipe line.
Nothing, for little things grow."

For more than two decades Standard Oil had batted aside
any would-be challengers with a mixture of strategies and tactics that would have made Sun Tzu nod his head in approval.
In this respect, the Standard was actually in a slightly a different category than the trusts built by J. P. Morgan. If Morgan
used carrots—splitting the proceeds of monopoly—Rockefeller preferred a big stick—the exclusionary cartel, ruinous
railroad prices, predatory refining prices, and the passage of
laws designed to exclude any would-be competitor. Rockefeller
liked to offer his smaller rivals the choice first popularized by
Genghis Khan: Join the empire, or face complete destruction.

60   In fact, the continued existence of Standard Oil threatened to make a mockery of the antitrust law. For if the law would tolerate Standard Oil, the original trust, an abusive monopoly, how could it be said to be an "anti" trust law at all?

Roosevelt, as we've said, was determined to demonstrate that government was sovereign over even the mightiest corporations, even Standard Oil. But Roosevelt was politically savvy enough to understand that he needed an angle. His opportunity was created by the publication, in 1904, of a sensational and widely read history of Standard Oil in *McClure's* magazine by reporter Ida Tarbell.

The History of the Standard Oil Company, nineteen parts in total, was a product of extensive reporting, and it told the full story of both Standard Oil's rise to power and its quashing of threats to its rule. Carefully researched and written in a balanced fashion, yet dark in its implications, the series reached a large audience and provoked national outrage. Tarbell discovered and documented previously unknown abuses—particularly, in the use of railroad rates—and revealed a certain darkness at the heart of the trust. Here is an example of an exchange she published:

> "But we don't want to sell," objected Mr. Hanna [an independent refiner.]
>
> "You can never make any more money, in my judgment," said Mr. Rockefeller. "You can't compete with the Standard. We have all the large refineries now. If you refuse to sell, it will end in your being crushed."

Among the objections to the Trust movement, as we've seen with Brandeis, was the observation that the drive to bigness and monopoly also seemed inevitably to come with its own morality, one that either displaced or replaced Christian or other moral strictures, at least for matters of business. But the drives toward monopoly were rough affairs, inevitably demanding a departure from practices previously considered moral or ethical in personal dealings. They tended to involve deception, bribery, and manipulation, and at worst, sabotage, bankrupting of rivals, and even the killing of workers to quell unrest.

The trusts seemed to come with a new system—a "dual morality," which arguably came to its fullest flower later in the writings of novelist Ayn Rand. It was a morality that would come to celebrate brutality in commerce, and the holding of one set of ethical or moral rules for personal dealings, and another very different set of rules for business. Indeed they were sometimes quite the opposite: The more extreme the piety of personal views, the more extreme the commercial abuses.

Tarbell noticed exactly this tendency in John D. Rockefeller. As she wrote "there was no more faithful baptist in Cleveland than he . . . He gave to its poor. He visited its sick." And yet "he was willing to strain every nerve . . . to ruin every man in the oil business." She felt that "religious emotion and sentiments of charity . . . seem to have taken the place in him of notions of justice and regard for the rights of others."

The split personality characteristic of this dual morality was if anything more acute in J. P. Morgan. "A man always has two reasons for the things he does," Morgan once told an associate. "A good one and the real one." At home in New York, he was a pious family man who attended church twice on Sundays. He was the senior warden of St. George's Church in Manhattan, and in his will he described his soul as free of sin. Yet while

62   overseas or aboard his massive steamship yacht, *The Corsair,* he
seemed to adopt a completely different set of ethics, enjoying
cruder pursuits, cutting secret deals to bankrupt rivals, bribing
government officials, and enriching himself and friends. He
also enjoyed a steady stream of female visitors on his ship, and
maintained a well-documented collection of mistresses, many
of whom seem to have been well-compensated for their attention to such a strikingly ugly man. At times, he seemed to have
more freely mixed his interests in religion with his playboy life-
style. While cruising down the Nile at age seventy-four, his
"party had included, characteristically, a bishop and several
attractive ladies." The latter (and maybe the former) he show-
ered with gold jewelry purchased in Cairo—"help yourselves,"
he said.

Times have not changed so much, and business magnates
do not stand alone in compartmentalizing their morality. But
what was new were the lengths taken to justify certain conduct,
as opposed to hiding it, making the unethical into the necessary,
indeed the proper.

The revelation of Standard Oil's abuses was particularly
important for Roosevelt and his approach to enforcement.
For the story of Roosevelt the trustbuster is the simple story,
and the simple story is sometimes the more important one. It
unquestionably describes Roosevelt in his first term. But as we
have hinted, Roosevelt was, in fact, far more conflicted about
the antitrust laws then he liked to let on. For while thought that
the trusts needed to brought to heel, made accountable to the
public, he also worshiped size and power as much as any man.
The early Roosevelt made peace with his internal contradic-
tions using a simple but vitally important distinction: a line

between the "bad trusts" and the "good trusts." In other words,   63
he would bust only the bad trusts, those engaged in abuse of
competitors, corruption of politic process, and general villainy.
But, as he put it "we grudge no man a fortune which represents
his own power and sagacity" he said, if "exercised with entire
regard to the welfare of his fellows...."*

Given an opening by Tarbell, and with the patience of a
hunter, President Roosevelt directed his newly created Bureau
of Corporations (the predecessor of the Federal Trade Commission) to investigate Standard Oil's practices. After two years of
fact-finding, Roosevelt transmitted a report to Congress, echoing
Tarbell's findings but going deeper, offering a damning account of
abuse of competitors over a long time. Having cornered his opponent, Roosevelt announced that his Justice Department would
now be taking up the question of prosecution.

What had Standard Oil done, according to investigators
and the courts? While the record is lengthy, we can concen-
trate on two main periods. Over the 1870s Rockefeller monopolized oil refining, and did so not just by growing, but through a
mixture of exclusionary cartels, the leverage of railroad pricing
power, and a bold program of acquisitions. Rockefeller began

---

*The idea of a simple line between the good and bad monopolist may seem too
simplistic for such a vital question but it is also not necessarily easy to improve
upon. If we leap forward to consider the tech monopolies of our times, we can
see that the good/bad question is inescapable. More than a hundred years
later, a version of Roosevelt's line remains the centerpiece of the U.S. Supreme
Court's test for assessing whether monopolization violates the Sherman Act,
albeit in much drier, lawyerly language. The test, from *United States v. Grin-
nell*, condemns "the willful acquisition or maintenance of [monopoly] power
as distinguished from growth or development as a consequence of a superior
product, business acumen, or historic accident."

64   by banding together with the other large refiners in Cleveland and Pittsburgh, and they collectively struck a deal with the major railroads that guaranteed lower rates for their shipments while fixing prices higher for anyone out of the club—that is, would-be independents or smaller competitors.* This part of his strategy exactly reflects today's battles over Net Neutrality, for Rockefeller used the key economic network of his time (the railroads) to ensure a major disadvantage for his smaller rivals. The cartel system was discovered and illegalized, but Rockefeller and his allies turned to secret "rebates" on railroad prices with the same effect. Eventually most of the states and the federal government enacted common carriage law, which mandated charging standardized carriage rates, but Standard Oil still found ways to secretly violate the law.

The exclusionary railroad cartel had more than one purpose, for it also served as a club. Rockefeller embarked on an industry shakeout, using the threat of higher railroad rates to begin forcing smaller refineries to sell out to him at a loss. Once he'd bought out his smaller rivals, he turned on his larger partners as well, bringing them all into a single trust under his control. In just over a decade, Rockefeller drove the market share of Standard Oil from 10 percent to over 90 percent.

Building a monopoly is one thing, but Standard Oil then managed to defend the monopoly and its profits for the next

---

*Why would the railroads agree to the plan (which after all, lowered their prices)? Given the collective bargaining power of the major refineries, they may have given them little choice. But the deal also gave them guaranteed volume, and perhaps the opportunity to ward off their own competitors. In later years, Rockefeller would take substantial ownership interests in the railroads, which may have later played a factor.

thirty years, even in the face of disruptive new technologies, like the oil pipeline, which, as many important technologies do, threatened to bring new competition and lower prices to the industry. Rockefeller identified and met the challenge of pipelines directly, by building his own and ensuring the ruin of his new pipeline challengers. He prevented many pipelines from being built in the first place, or bankrupted and acquired those that managed to be built, a process that tended to scare off would-be competitors. Among the tactics used to keep competitors at bay were regionalized pricing strategies (strategically overpaying for crude in some markets, lowering prices in others), and the assertion of political influence, such as ensuring that government would prevent rival pipelines from getting the rights-of-way they might need or even banning competing pipelines altogether. Contrary to revisionist history, "predatory pricing" was not the only or the main method used by Standard Oil; it mastered the many ways of fighting dirty to keep its grip on the industry.*

Armed with copious evidence of these various abuses and exclusions, the Justice Department filed a 170-page complaint in 1906. Among various behaviors indicted were the exclusive cartel deals with the railroads, abuse of its pipeline monopoly,

---

*A longstanding revisionist history suggests that Standard Oil was a more efficient refiner that was unfairly condemned for having "lower prices." Support comes from a 1958 study by economic historian John McGee, who concluded that Standard Oil had not, in fact, been proved to engage in below-cost pricing. (1 J. L. & Econ. 137.) Yet in fact Standard Oil relied on a menu of exclusionary tactics, not just predatory pricing, to gain and maintain monopoly. In 2012, Christopher Leslie reexamined the data relied upon by McGee, finding both distortions and also new data suggesting that the Standard did, indeed, price below cost. (85 S. Cal. L. Rev. 573.)

66 and predatory pricing—conduct that, to the ears of a contemporary antitrust lawyer, violates the ban on monopolization (Section 2 of the Sherman Act), and restraints on trade (Section 1 of the Sherman Act).

With this the stage was set, but one thing is important to know, for it portended the future. Roosevelt, just before pulling the trigger, summoned Standard Oil's leadership to the White House for a secret meeting. There he put a different option into consideration: Might the world's largest oil company be willing to accept government oversight, promise to clean up their act, and even, perhaps, become the first "public" trust?

This offer reflected the fact that Roosevelt's primary concern was not so much decentralization, but the supremacy of elected government. It was an interesting possibility—imagine the United States government in active control of the world's largest oil company, now reformed to serve as a public utility. In some ways, it might have made the United States more like Saudi Arabia, where Saudi Aramco, the state-controlled oil company, forms a major part of the economy, and currently has an estimated value of some $1.4 to $2.1 trillion (in comparison, Apple, the world's most valuable public company, is worth $1 trillion). But this alternative history was not to pass, because Standard Oil rebuffed him entirely. It would be many years until another firm said "yes" to a similar offer—AT&T, the telephone monopolist. In any case, facing mounting evidence of villainy, Roosevelt adjudged Standard Oil to be what he called a "bad trust" and decided it was time, again, to go to war.

In the summer of 1906, President Roosevelt and the cabinet unanimously agreed to bring suit against Standard Oil. By that time, Standard Oil also faced a flurry of state antitrust actions, as well as an investigation into railroad rate manipulation that made criminal prosecution possible. The case went to trial, and 1,371 exhibitions were entered into evidence, while the government called 444 witnesses. The lower courts adjudged Standard Oil guilty, and faced with overwhelming evidence, it was not particularly hard for the Supreme Court to conclude in 1911 that Standard Oil was the kind of abusive and anti-competitive trust that the Sherman Act had been designed to illegalize. The Court, most importantly, affirmed the remedy: a breakup of the firm into some 34 constituent parts.

Among scholars, and among its critics, the Supreme Court's decision is usually remarked upon for its implication that only "unreasonable" restraints of trade or combinations were illegal. That dictum was undoubtedly important. It set up one of the greatest questions for antitrust: are all monopolies forbidden, or only the "abusive" among them? In Roosevelt's usage, did the law ban all trusts, or just "bad trusts?" But this much was clear: A monopoly with a track record of exclusion and abuse like Standard Oil warranted the dissolution of the firm.

Justice Harlan concurred in the dissolution of Standard Oil, but was incensed by the Court's implicit holding that a "reasonable" conduct might not be condemned. In memorable fashion, he restated the origins and purposes of the Sherman Act:

All who recall the condition of the country in 1890 will remember that there was everywhere, among the people generally, a deep feeling of unrest. The nation had been rid of human slavery, fortunately, as all now feel—but the conviction was universal that the country was in real danger from another kind of slavery sought to be fastened on the American people; namely, the slavery that would result from aggregations of capital in the hands of a few individuals and corporations controlling, for their own profit and advantage exclusively, the entire business of the country, including the production and sale of the necessaries of life. Such a danger was thought to be then imminent, and all felt that it must be met firmly and by such statutory regulations as would adequately protect the people against oppression and wrong.

Economies and *Diseconomies* of Scale

Standard Oil was broken into its constituents parts, among them seven "majors," many of which remain among the most valuable and powerful firms on Earth, including, notably, Standard Oil of New Jersey (Exxon), Standard Oil of New York (Mobil), and Standard Oil of California (Chevron). In the aftermath of the breakup, stock was divided proportionately, and, to the surprise of many observers, within a year, the value of what had been Standard Oil had doubled, and in several years, had increased five-fold.

The story of Standard Oil raises what is perhaps the central economic question we shall confront. The proponents of the trust argued that their size and monopoly control was natural and necessary: that the larger firm was simply more efficient than the small operators of old. The economic phrase that captures this idea is that of "economies of scale," and it simply suggests that larger producers will outperform smaller ones. If this is true, is the whole enterprise of antitrust and decentralization misguided?

Let us examine this question carefully. It is true that a large factory, operating at volume, will usually produce goods at lower cost than a mom-and-pop operation. That's why cars are produced on large assembly lines, not at the neighborhood craft automobile manufacturer. It is something also witnessed in the tech world. In the age of Amazon and Google it often seems that the company which has the most servers or collects the most data necessarily has the better product.

But the economics of the last century have made it clear that the basic proposition—that bigger is better—is subject to both limitations and caveats that make the full picture complex. First, at some point, economies of scale "run out"—that is, increasing size no longer creates further efficiencies. A car plant needs to be a certain size to be efficient, but after that, it no longer becomes any more efficient. That point varies by product and industry. Making pizza efficiently requires little more than an industrial oven, giving a massive operation no efficiency advantage over a neighborhood store. The advantages, if any, are those related to size, power, reputation, and so on—compare the Domino's chain to the local pizzeria—but are not actually related to the ability to make a better product.

The size problem is made more complex by two more factors. One is that as the size of the operation increases, "dis-economies" of scale begin to creep in, as economists since Alfred Marshall in the 1920s have suggested. For example, as a firm adds more and more employees, it needs to add more managers, and ever-more complex systems of internal control, which tend, at some point, to begin making the firm less

70 efficient. Managers in larger firms may start to yield to the temptations of seeking their own personal enrichment and power as opposed to the interests of the firm. Sometimes great size yields a short-term advantage, but creates "dynamic" disadvantages: A larger firm may also become cumbersome, unable to adapt to changing market conditions. Consider that General Motors was thought a paragon of efficiency in the 1950s, but by the 1980s had become an unwieldy monster that eventually went bankrupt.

Hence the premise that productive efficiency usually has a U-shaped relationship with scale, as pictured here:

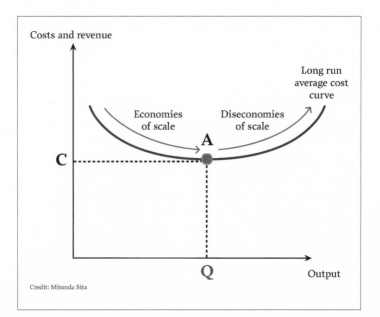

Credit: Miranda Sita

This is the curse of bigness illustrated. The point is intuitive to anyone who has actually worked in an enormous organization of some age and wondered where the phrase "efficiencies of scale" could have come from. As business tycoon T. Boone Pickens once put it, "It's unusual to find a large corporation that's efficient. I know about economies of scale and all the other advantages that are supposed to come with size. But when you get an inside look, it's easy to see how inefficient big business really is."*

It was these creeping inefficiencies in sprawling firms that Brandeis thought of as comprising part of the curse of bigness. But there is another side to the curse, one associated with growing power. It is this: As a business gets larger, it begins to enjoy a different kind of advantages having less to do with efficiencies of operation, and more to do with its ability to wield economic and political power, by itself or conjunction with others. In other words, a firm may not actually become more efficient as it gets larger, but may become better at raising prices or keeping out competitors.

---

*If an oversized firm starts to suffer from the curse of bigness, why would a firm ever grow past its optimal size? This is not mysterious to any student of empire, or of human ambition; in contemporary economic theory it is usually described, as representing the difference between the interests of the corporation and its management. The owners of a corporation, the shareholders, may prefer a smaller profitable operation, but executives and founders prefer to run a great empire and conquer their rivals, an ambition that can easily overcome any effort to have a firm that operates at "efficient" size. As economist Michael Jensen, a founder of "agency theory" dryly explains: "Managers have incentives to cause their firms to grow beyond the optimal size" because "growth increases managers' power by increasing the resources under their control."

72   The large firm, alone or in cooperation, can and usually does invest in "moats"—the business school term for barriers that are designed to keep out new competitors who might have better-quality products or cheaper prices. There are myriad methods of doing so—like control of scarce resources, exclusive or preferential deals with retailers or distributors, government licenses, and so.

Meanwhile, the growth of individual firms through mergers usually correlates with increased "concentration"—that is, fewer firms in the industry. And once an industry is composed of just a few majors, it becomes easier for them to jointly extract a cost to society. The easy way is by coordinating on higher prices. The fewer members in the industry, the easier it is to cooperate on building a "joint moat"—perhaps the "walled city" is a better metaphor—designed to keep out any would-be invaders. Finally, as we have seen, giant firms, often in cooperation with their counterparts, have great incentives to invest in the political process to obtain the passage of laws that either fortify the moat or just transfer wealth to the industry, like tax cuts or subsidies.

The effects of size and concentration are not limited to mere self-preservation. The larger and more powerful firm has a clearer bargaining advantage over its workers; the monopolist most of all. Back in the nineteenth century, the power of large firms enabled them to drive workers harder and longer, for less money, and also provided the resources to break unions with violent attacks, sometimes by even hiring their own armed militias. Today, concentrated economic power is used to avoid raising wages, to insist on intense conditions of employment, to abuse of "non-compete" agreements, and to hire part-timers

instead of full-time employees. The more power a firm or
industry enjoys, the easier it is to prevent employees from getting too much of the returns.

To be sure, there are some private checks on bigness, or of
the building of empire for empire's sake. The firm's owners or
board of directors may order management to stop expanding for
no good reason but their own welfare. Smaller, more efficient
competitors do sometimes manage to kill a bloated dinosaur, or
the firm may be taken over by a corporate raider who sees value
in breaking the firm into smaller pieces. But unfortunately,
these market-based checks on bigness can and do fail, and their
mythology can outmatch their real effectiveness. For they are,
at all times, counterbalanced by the advantages and attractions
of power, and the allure of monopoly profit. For that reason,
oversized, inefficient firms can persist for decades, effectively
immunized from the need to improve products or lower prices.
Instead, like American domestic airlines, the industry can happily offer a product that continues to get worse and cost more.

That monopoly can be an inefficient form was a lesson
from the Standard Oil case, for in the end, the breakup of the
oil industry was a boon to its further expansion. That isn't
unusual: the break-up of the original film-trust sparked the
rise of the American film industry; and in more recent times the
campaigns against AT&T and IBM sparked a momentous boom
in the telecommunications and computing industries. The cries
of doom, gloom and economic catastrophe are often overblown,
for some industries can benefit from a breakup. Indeed, as the
example of the Standard suggests, while the patient may protest, the government is sometimes doing it a favor.

74   **Antitrust's Constitutional Moment**

Roosevelt's cases against Standard Oil and J. P. Morgan were his most dramatic; but in total, he filed forty-five cases and achieved numerous breakups. The trustbusting campaign continued under his successor, President William Howard Taft, who pursued a total of seventy-five cases, including cases targeting U.S. Steel and AT&T, two of J. P. Morgan's other creations. By the end of the 1910s, just about every one of the major trusts had been broken into pieces or had some encounter with the antitrust law, making it, for a while at least, a primary level of federal economic policymaking. In this sense Roosevelt achieved his goal—demonstrating the primacy of the elected government over the structure of the economy.

However, as we've already said, Roosevelt's views of monopoly and size were more complex that the trustbuster moniker allows. He had an incurable admiration for that which was grand, mighty, and powerful, like the new U.S. Navy he helped build. He could not help feeling affection for the sheer power of big businesses, but at the same time he believed that elected government must be sovereign over business.

In his earlier years, Roosevelt's faith in law enforcement won the day, but in his later years he lost patience. When running for president in 1912 as the head of his own party, Roosevelt became the advocate of a different approach—one then new to American history, but with a difficult legacy in the twentieth century. Roosevelt campaigned on a platform he called "New Nationalism," where he promised not to break up, but to nationalize or supervise the remaining trust monopolies. In other words, Roosevelt proposed abandoning the very idea of a competitive or decentralized economy, in favor of one dominated by monopolists who were then, in turn, subject to the direction and regulation of the state—the paradigm of "regulated monopoly." Roosevelt's approach, later termed "corporatism" by political scientists, was at some level not really so different from the Crown monopolies loyal to the British King, nor, as we discuss more in a moment, was it that much different than the corporate-state alliances adopted by Japan, Germany, and Italy in the 1930s.

There was more here than a rejection of antitrust: It was a rejection of the entire idea of a competitive economy, and that is what makes the 1912 election so important to our story. With Roosevelt and the socialist candidate Eugene Debs both calling for state-supervised monopolies, it became one of the few elections in history where the public was clearly engaged with and voting on what kind of economic order they wished to live in. On the one hand, here was candidate Roosevelt promising a future of monopolies supervised by an all-powerful federal government—as he said, "to give the National Government complete power over the organization and capitalization of all business concerns." On the other, Taft, the Republican, and Wilson, the Democrat, both promised to restore a competitive economy by fighting the trusts with the antitrust law and new regulations—ironically, doubling down on the model Roosevelt himself pioneered. Debs, the socialist candidate, called the antitrust law "silly" and "puerile," for he believed in an economy composed of monopolies controlled by the people. As he put it, "Monopoly is certain and sure. It is merely a question of whether we will be collectively owned monopolies, for the good of the race, or whether they will be privately owned for the

76 power, pleasure, and glory of the Morgans, Rockefellers, Guggenheims, and Carnegies."

It is interesting to speculate on how the history of the United States might have turned out had Roosevelt won. Perhaps it would have amounted in the end to little more than the selective nationalization of most of their public utility and telecommunications providers practiced by other Western democracies like Britain and France. But Roosevelt had promised to go further, to accept regulated monopolies across the entire economy, suggesting something similar to the extreme approaches taken by the Italian and German governments over the 1930s. What Roosevelt was proposing amounted to a union of political and economic power unknown even to the greatest of ancient emperors. All commerce would be controlled by a small group of monopolists, who would be, in turn, controlled by government (or perhaps vice versa). If Roosevelt had won the 1912 election, and managed to enact his program, the history of the United States would have been profoundly different, and probably far darker, given the fact that such cooperation was so closely linked to the rise of fascism in other countries. Unfortunately, the monopolist and dictator tend to have overlapping interests.

But Woodrow Wilson won the 1912 election, based on economic and antitrust policies directly taken from Louis Brandeis, his economic advisor—which the latter labeled "regulated competition." The Roosevelt-Debs proposal of supervised monopolies was not popular: the competing candidates took some 65 percent of the popular vote.

After Wilson's victory, Congress proceeded to fortify the antitrust laws with a series of new statutes. The Clayton Act of 1914 ratified and toughened the Sherman Act and explicitly criminalized particular anticompetitive practices. That same year, Congress created a specialized competition and consumer protection agency named the Federal Trade Commission and gave it powers to investigate and bring suit against any "unfair methods of competition."* The importance of these new laws lies not just in their specific provisions, but in their democratic resolution of the uncertainty surrounding the purpose of the Sherman Act. The new laws were a Congressional ratification of the view that the antitrust laws were meant not to be merely symbolic, or just to benefit small producers or consumers. When we add up the popular vote for President and the subsequent passage of stronger antitrust laws in 1914 it becomes clear that the Wilson-Brandeis economic antitrust program enjoyed a powerful democratic validation—one arguably of Constitutional significance.†

In short, in the 1910s, it is fair to say that the United States made a choice. As Brandeis would later say, the nation had picked decentralization over concentration, and competition over monopoly. That choice has never been repealed, by democratic means anyhow.

---

*The originally intended role of the Federal Trade Commission has always been slightly unclear. Historian Gerald Berk argues persuasively that Brandeis wanted the FTC to facilitate a middle ground between ruinous competition and monopolization—so-called "regulated competition." See Gerald Berk, *Louis D. Brandeis and the Making of Regulated Competition, 1900–1932* (2009).

†Based on the theory, popularized by Bruce Ackerman, that the Constitution undergoes de facto amendments during times of intense popular attention to questions of Constitutional significance. See Bruce A. Ackerman, *We the People, Vol. 1: Foundations* (1991).

Peak Antitrust and the Chicago School

It was during the postwar years, over the 1950s and 1960s, that strong antitrust laws became most clearly identified as part of a functional democracy, and in that sense reached the fullest extent of their power, influence, and political support. Reflecting the mood, President Kennedy's antitrust chief, Lee Loevinger, would testify before Congress as follows: "The problems with which the antitrust laws are concerned—the problems of distribution of power within society—are second only to the questions of survival in the face of threats of nuclear weapons." As he told Robert Kennedy in a job interview, "I believe in antitrust almost as a secular religion."

The road to peak antitrust was not entirely smooth. The laws did suffer a near-death experience in the early 1930s, at a time when nationalization and central planning were in fashion around the world. During FDR's first New Deal, Congress effectively suspended the laws in a failed effort to generate economic recovery.* But the law began its recovery under a succession of prominent and effective Neo-Brandeisians, including Robert Jackson, the future Supreme Court Justice, and the legendary Thurman Arnold, the Wyoming Cowboy, who inherited Theodore Roosevelt's trustbuster mantle, and who brought about a "shock treatment" campaign amounting to an astonishing 1,375 complaints in 213 cases involving 40 industries.†

But the real political support for the laws in the postwar period came from the fact that they were understood as a bulwark against the terrifying examples of Japan, Italy, and most of all the Third Reich. As antitrust scholar Daniel Crane writes, "the post-War currents of democracy-enhancing antitrust ideology arose in the United States and Europe in reaction to the role that concentrated economic power played in stimulating the rise of fascism." Thurman Arnold was more blunt: "Germany became organized to such an extent that a Fuehrer was inevitable; had it not been Hitler it would have been someone else."

---

*The National Recovery Act of 1933 allowed industries to submit their own codes of competition, and offered an exemption from the antitrust laws in exchange.

†The law also received a boost from the famous *Alcoa* decision, a condemnation of the persistent aluminum monopoly written by judge Learned Hand. In *Alcoa*, Hand articulated a better repudiation of monopoly than Brandeis himself had ever managed, writing that a "possession of unchallenged economic power deadens initiative, discourages thrift, and depresses energy; that immunity from competition is a narcotic, and rivalry is a stimulant, to industrial progress; that the spur of constant stress is necessary to counteract an inevitable disposition to let well enough alone." Congress, said Hand, had chosen to "prefer a system of small producers, each dependent for his success upon his own skill and character, to one in which the great mass of those engaged must accept the direction of a few."

80   Hitler's rise and exercise of power were facilitated by the German Republic's tolerance of monopolies in key industries, including the Krupp armaments company, Siemens railroad and infrastructure, and, most of all, the I.G. Farben chemical cartel. As a report by the Secretary of War concluded: "Germany under the Nazi set-up built up a great series of industrial monopolies in steel, rubber, coal, and other materials. The monopolies soon got control of Germany, brought Hitler to power, and forced virtually the whole world into war." That conclusion came from the observation that the main German monopolists, over the 1930s, threw their weight behind the Nazi regime when it lacked support among other key groups, and that each ultimately became deeply allied with and enmeshed in the German war effort. As a U.S. military report concluded in 1945, I.G. Farben became "a colossal empire serving the German State as one of the principal industrial cores around which successive German drives for world conquest have been organized." Ultimately some twenty-four Farben executives were tried for war crimes at Nuremberg, for practicing human enslavement in occupied territories, among other offenses. As for I.G. Farben, it was subject to an American style breakup into nine firms, including three large ones: Bayer, Hoechst, and BASF.*

---

* American war efforts had also been hindered by a series of international cartel agreements in areas like synthetic rubber and aluminum that became essential to the buildup of American forces. There had been, as the *New Republic* alleged, "a Corporate International, joining the Communist International and Fascist International, seeking to undermine the free world." The cartels were alleged to be part of Germany's plan for world domination. German-run international cartels, the theory went, limited production while Germany prepared for war, part of an alleged "Peace at Düsseldorf."

Concerns that excessive corporate concentration under-
mined democracy prompted Congress to once again strengthen
the antitrust laws, in a new "Anti-Merger Act." Politically, the
law was explicitly styled as a reaction to the German and Soviet
examples. As Senator Estes Kefauver put it:

> I think we must decide very quickly what sort of country we
> want to live in. The present trend of great corporations to
> increase their economic power is the antithesis of meritorious
> competitive development . . . Through monopolistic mergers
> the people are losing power to direct their own economic wel-
> fare. When they lose the power to direct their economic wel-
> fare they also lose the means to direct their political future.

He then turned to antitrust's relationship to democracy.

> I am not an alarmist, but the history of what has taken place in
> other nations where mergers and concentrations have placed
> economic control in the hands of a very few people is too clear
> to pass over easily. A point is eventually reached, and we are rap-
> idly reaching that point in this country, where the public steps
> in to take over when concentration and monopoly gain too much
> power. The taking over by the public through its government
> always follows one or two methods and has one or two political
> results. It either results in a Fascist state or the nationalization
> of industries and thereafter a Socialist or Communist state.

The Anti-Merger Act, nicknamed the "Celler–Kefauver
Act," passed by large majorities in 1950, and gave the government new tools to prevent the buildup of giants firms in advance,
by controlling—or undoing—mergers. Instead of trying to break

82 up the giants decades later, its idea was to prevent their formation in the first place. The Justice Department and the Federal
Trade Commission now had a powerful new tool for controlling
bigness—one that was, in fact, potentially the most powerful.

It was over the same period that the European Community
(predecessor to the European Union) adopted its own antitrust,
or competition, system, modeled on the American Sherman
Act.* As in the United States, it too was backed not just by the
sense that the law would facilitate economic development, but
also the belief that breaking up monopolies and prohibiting cartels was essential to democratic governance, human thriving,
and a prevention of a return to the despotism of the 1930s and
1940s. The new European laws found support with an intellectual movement, the Ordoliberals, originally a German school
that had faced repression during the Nazi-era based on its belief
in economic freedoms. The Ordoliberal beliefs aligned closely
with those of the Neo-Brandesians—with a commitment to
free markets operating within a strong social, political, and
moral framework. Like Thurman Arnold, Estes Kefauver, and
other Americans, the Ordoliberals believed that the true origins
of Nazi totalitarianism were the concentrations of economic
power that began under Bismarck. In this sense, the European
competition law was entwined, from the beginning, to the commitment to democracy and human freedom.

*In contrast, efforts to transplant U.S. antitrust laws to Japan during the
same period were not particularly successful. The U.S. occupation authority
forced passage of an antitrust law, and created an agency to enforce it, but
the law was overshadowed by the economic planning practiced by other
agencies. See Etsuko Kameoka, *Competition Law and Policy in Japan and The
EU* (2014), pp. 5–6

By the 1960s, the antitrust laws and an anti-concentration mandate were broadly accepted as part of a functioning democracy. To be sure, the laws had become far more complex and technocratic, and no longer the subject of a popular movement, nor were they the subject of contested electoral politics, as in the 1912 election.* But a broad political, legal, and intellectual consensus saw excessive economic concentration and monopolization as both economically dubious and politically dangerous.

However, a new intellectual opposition to antitrust was brewing, in a different form than before, and in an unexpected place. It formed at the University of Chicago, the school founded by John D. Rockefeller, and in the person of a professor named Aaron Director, and a particularly brilliant student of his named Robert Bork.

The Rise of the Chicago School

Since at least Adam Smith's day, economists have favored competition and condemned monopoly. For most of the twentieth century, antitrust enforcement was, therefore, broadly supported by the economic profession in its home country. As Donald Dewey writes, "not a single American-trained economist of any prominence questioned the desirability of antitrust in the interwar years." Given this baseline, the fact that mainstream antitrust economics would come to tolerate and even celebrate monopoly makes for an extraordinary tale.

---

*In the early 1960s, historian Richard Hofstadter would famously remark that antitrust was no longer a popular movement but that it "now runs its quiet course without much public attention."

84   By the postwar period, when antitrust reached its heights, there remained strong intellectual backing for antitrust laws among both conservative and liberal economists.* Liberal economists tended to support antitrust as a counter to the domination of big business. Conservatives feared "a road to serfdom," in Friedrich Hayek's phrase, resulting from central planning accomplished through a union of monopolies and the state. Some thought of monopolies as a threat to economic freedom by themselves; others feared that private monopolies provided an excuse for nationalization or at least extensive regulation. Here is conservative economist George Stigler, writing in 1952: "The dissolution of big businesses is . . . a part of the program necessary to increase the support for a private, competitive enterprise economy, and reverse the drift toward government control."

A far more obscure man named Aaron Director would lead the economic attack that would later become known as the Chicago School of Antitrust. Director, who taught at the University of Chicago law school, but was neither a lawyer, nor an economist with a PhD, was a mysterious Socrates-like figure who left behind few written works, but whose students were many and whose intellectual influence over late-twentieth-century legal thought is matched by few. Born in the Russian empire, Director

*One prominent exception was the iconoclastic economist Joseph Schumpeter, who had championed the entrepreneur in his earlier years, but in his later years grew to admire the large monopolistic corporation and begun to see the lure of monopoly as a principal driver of innovation and "creative destruction." Schumpeter, however, did not take seriously the problem of investment in barriers to entry, and particularly the power of government to insulate monopolies from creative destruction. See Tim Wu, *The Master Switch* (2010).

grew up in Portland, Oregon, and was a onetime leftist-socialist. At Yale, he published a socialist newspaper with his friend, artist Mark Rothko. Over the 1930s, he moved to the right, and by the 1950s, he was co-teaching antitrust law at the University of Chicago.

Director's big idea was brilliant in its simplicity. Working with classic price theories (that, at the time, had been discarded as unrealistic by most of the economic profession), he attacked Supreme Court case law as insensitive or counterproductive in terms of "consumer welfare." By this he meant the measure of whether the economic prospects of the consumer were enhanced in a measurable way, which usually meant evidence of lower prices. The goal of preserving competition might simply protect weaker, less efficient companies from more efficient firms that might lower prices for consumers.

Director may have started alone, more or less, but he soon gained an impressive band of followers and associates. He was an exceptionally inspirational teacher and colleague, who prompted great loyalty and admiration. He influenced students and colleagues like John McGee (who attacked the Standard Oil decision), Ward Bowman ("Tying Arrangements and the Leverage Problem"), and future federal judges Robert Bork, Richard Posner, and Frank Easterbrook. To various degrees they tended to share Director's method and assumptions. As McGee once put it, one must begin with "the strongest presumption that the existing structure is the efficient structure." In other words, they began with a presumption that antitrust was unnecessary, based on the *laissez-faire* idea that problems work themselves out, and most of the time we live in the best of all possible worlds.

86   The Chicago School struck some important and worthy blows. Director encouraged McGee, then a graduate student, to study "predatory" pricing in the Standard Oil case, and if McGee's historical work has been questioned since, it was worth asking when government should be challenging the strategy of lowering prices to defeat competitors, given that lower prices are also a means of competing on price. Perhaps Chicago's most successful shots, however, were taken at the Supreme Court's categorical, or *per se*, condemnation of "vertical agreements"—that is, agreements between producers and retailers. Total bans on such arrangements were hard to justify, and even Louis Brandeis was among the critics of them. Vertical-agreement rules would prove the easiest targets for the Chicago School's attack.

Nonetheless, even by the mid-1960s, Director and his adherents remained in what Richard Posner would later call "the lunatic fringe," and their views were not considered important enough to merit inclusion in mainstream legal or academic summaries of antitrust laws. Moreover, Director's critiques were external; he faulted the law based on what he thought the law's goals should be ("consumer welfare"), not what they were, like the scientist who faults *Star Wars* for failing to explain hyperspace. To become influential, what Director actually needed was a lawyer—someone who could weaponize his ideas, put them in a form usable by attorneys and judges. Fortunately for him, he would find his advocate in the greatest and most loyal of his students.

Robert Bork was born in Pittsburgh and grew up in the suburb of Ben Avon. His father was in the steel industry, and his mother was a teacher. Sometime in his youth, he surprised his parents and classmates by declaring himself a socialist, and remained loyal to that cause throughout college. Bork had originally thought he'd be a journalist and writer, in the model of Ernest Hemingway; like Hemingway, he liked to box, and he also made an effort to join the Marines at the end of the Second World War.

During law school, Bork began to soften politically, becoming what he called a "New Deal" liberal. And so things were, and might have stayed, until Bork took an antitrust class co-taught by Aaron Director. During that semester, he underwent what he later called a "religious conversion." As Bork later said, "Aaron gradually destroyed my dreams of socialism with price theory." He would become a self-described "janissary," or loyal soldier, for Director.

As the switch from socialism to free-market libertarianism suggests, Bork dwelt in the extremes, preferring strong positions, which he stated with eloquence and confidence. And unlike Director or other Chicago School economists, he was a first-rate legal talent as well. In this respect he was equaled only by Richard Posner, but the latter never had the same singlemindedness and bombast that Bork did, nor anything like Bork's inflexibility. While Posner would prove influential over a range of fields, and widely respected for his thoughtful and far-ranging mind, Bork was far more of a soldier: He advanced his position and marched forward without concession or regret, like the tank commander, leaving behind many critics, but also changing minds.

Bork's signal contribution was this. He took Director's "consumer welfare" idea—that antitrust was intended only to lower prices for consumers—and argued that it was not merely

88   what an economist like Director thought the law *should* do, but that it had been, all along, the *actual intent* of the laws. Working with his Chicago allies, he then created a fully formed alternative account of what the antitrust laws should do and not do, in a book entitled *The Antitrust Paradox*. In 1964, when he first presented the thesis, it was considered absurd and even insane. But within twenty years he'd manage to convince a majority of the Supreme Court to adopt his position.

How did Bork do it? The key was a 1966 paper, "Legislative Intent and the Policy of the Sherman Act," arguably the most influential single antitrust paper in history. There he conducted his own investigation of the debates surrounding the Sherman Act and arrived at an extraordinary conclusion. "Congress intended the courts to implement . . . only that value we would today call consumer welfare. To put it another way, the policy the courts were intended to apply is the maximization of wealth or consumer . . . satisfaction." In case that wasn't clear, he put it again this way: "The legislative history . . . contains no colorable support for application by courts of any value premise or policy other than the maximization of consumer welfare." Instead, Bork insisted, "courts should be guided exclusively by consumer welfare and the economic criteria which that value premise implies."

What did Bork mean by this exactly? He meant that in any antitrust case, the government or plaintiff had to prove to a certainty that the complained-of behavior actually raised *prices* for consumers. Consider Standard Oil, which, as we've seen, used a number of strategies and techniques to both destroy old competitors and keep out new ones. Not a problem, according to Bork, unless it could be proven that Standard Oil maintained higher prices or that those competitors would have actually lowered the price of heating oil. That approach to antitrust—the one, suspiciously enough, just invented by Aaron Director and his followers—had magically been in the minds of members of Congress in 1890 when they wrote the Sherman Act.

Absolute certainty in the face of much contradictory evidence is classic Bork. No other scholar ever managed to find what Bork did in the Congressional record. Bork relied heavily on the views of Senator Sherman, who did think the interests of buyers were important. However, Sherman had much broader concerns as well. He wanted antitrust law to fight "inequality of condition, of wealth, and opportunity" and feared that the trusts created "a kingly prerogative, inconsistent with our form of government." As Herbert Hovenkamp, today's reigning dean of antitrust doctrine, puts it: "Bork's analysis of the legislative history was strained, heavily governed by his own ideological agenda . . . . Not a single statement in the legislative history comes close to stating the conclusions that Bork drew."

Among other things, Bork's radically narrow reading of the Sherman Act threw out the broader concerns that had long animated the Act and its enforcement. Most important was the idea that grounds much of this book: that antitrust represented a democratic choice of economic structure and a check on the political and economic power of the monopolies. So was any regard for small producers. As Learned Hand had written, "It is possible, because of its indirect social or moral effect, to prefer a system of small producers, each dependent for his success upon his own skill and character, to one in which the great mass of those engaged must accept the direction of a few.

90 These considerations . . . prove to have been in fact [the law's] purposes."

Even within a strictly economic framework, Chicago was leaving much behind. The focus on "allocative efficiency" yielded almost no consideration of the "dynamic" costs of monopoly, like stagnation or stalled innovation. Virtues of competition stressed by Hayek, like the virtues of decentralizing information and the avoidance of central planning, were lost. Perhaps most surprising for a view inspired by economics was an approach to antitrust that was shockingly tolerant of monopoly, supposedly the economist's bête noire.

Given that Bork's singleminded interpretation was at odds with seventy years of precedent, as a legal matter his argument was dead on arrival. But over the years, Bork managed to skillfully tie Chicago School consumer welfare theories to another, very powerful legal locomotive that was just beginning its run by the late 1960s. By that point, concerns of "judicial activism" were no longer a liberal fear (as in the 1930s), but had become an important conservative trope. Bork repackaged his approach to antitrust as a tool of judicial restraint (not unlike "originalism," another of Bork's favorites). He insisted that the multiplicity of values served by antitrust was too vague, and served judicial irresponsibility, by allowing the judge to choose whatever value happened to match the judge's preordained result.* In Bork's critique, it seemed an antitrust law driven by anything

---

*In Bork's words: "A value will be announced as pertinent with a confidence that is matched only by the mystery that shrouds its derivation. A very specific decision is then whelped from the value premise without benefit of midwifery by any visible minor premise."

but consumer welfare was the law of the libertine, degenerate and debauched. Economic analysis was now righteous and self-restrained. As such, Bork managed to embed the culture war into one's method of interpreting the Sherman Act.

A final characteristic of Bork's approach was not merely to tap the culture war, but to offer judges a relatively easy way to deal with hard cases: They could eradicate messiness and complications in exchange for a simpler, disciplined, and single-pointed theory that yielded straightforward answers. This revealed an acute understanding of the judicial mind; despite the robes and bench, judges are still lawyers, and can become anxious when asked to decide complex and challenging cases. Bork offered a calming remedy, with an appealing simplicity and apparent rigor. For Bork's antitrust economics are *easy*—not easy enough for a schoolchild, but easy enough for a lawyer who does not specialize in antitrust and is looking for a dignified and respectable manner in which to decide, or get rid of, a hard case. The simple question that Bork posed for every doctrine was this: Does it clearly prevent harm to consumers? Have you proven it? Or might there, plausibly, be an economic explanation that doesn't imply harm, and if so, what is it? Hence Christopher Leslie's critique that "Bork's legacy is an oversimplified economics that often rests on unfounded or disproven assumptions."

In truth, clad in the costume of economic rigor, Robert Bork's attack on antitrust was really *laissez-faire* reincarnated, without the Social Darwinist baggage, and with a slightly less overt worship of monopoly—but with much the same results. With narrow exceptions, mainly related to price-fixing, the government was once again barred from trying to influence

92 economic structure, regardless of what Congress said or did. The belief that really mattered was that the market enjoyed its own sovereignty and was therefore necessarily immune from mere democratic politics. That meant that the antitrust law, which dared dictate what the economy should look like, needed be put into hibernation—perhaps forever.

The Last of the Big Cases

While the Chicago School gained vigor and strength over the 1970s, it would be wrong to imply that antitrust lawyers and judges woke up, read Bork's "Legislative Intent and the Policy of the Sherman Act," and hung up their hats. Instead, antitrust continued to run hot, clocking, along with some outlandish failures, some of its largest, most transformational cases. None was more so than the epic campaign against the dreadnought itself, the AT&T Corporation.

In the year 1974, AT&T was the largest firm on the planet, the employer of over a million people, and the uncontested holder of a monopoly that had, by then, lasted a full six decades. It was the most important and powerful incarnation of the corporatist vision—Morgan's creation; the colossus restrained, its activities carefully regulated by the Federal Communications Commission, under the banner of "regulated monopoly."

Life, in other words, was fine for the world's greatest blue whale, until 1974, when the Nixon White House announced a surprising change in policy. "Unless the would-be monopolist [AT&T] or the public can demonstrate a special public policy consideration that justifies monopoly, it should not be permitted." Later that same year, the Justice Department filed suits against AT&T, producing the largest and perhaps most consequential case in the entire history of the competition laws, resulting in the last massive breakup, and arguably the most successful in terms of its effect on the American economy, in the postwar era.

We should be a little more precise: AT&T was not the mere holder of a monopoly, but multiple monopolies—six or seven, depending on how one counts—making it the quintessential "super monopolist." At its height the firm controlled local telephone service, long distance service, the physical telephones, all other attachments, business telephone services, and markets just coming into existence, like "online" services.

Nowadays, even dominant firms pay at least lip service to the importance of competition. Not so AT&T, which even in its time was unusual in its ideological dedication to the principles of monopoly rule. Through the 1970s, it was still preaching the gospel of Morgan, celebrating the trust as a great human achievement, and denouncing "chaotic" and "ruinous" competition. That was a tone set by AT&T's first true ruler, Theodore Vail, who had made his reasoning moralistic: Competition was giving American business a bad name. "The vicious acts associated with aggressive competition are responsible for much, if not all, of the present antagonism in the public mind to business, particularly to large business."

Over the years, AT&T had not been content to be merely the neighborhood telephone monopolist. No, AT&T was the jealous

God of telecommunications, brooking no rivals, accepting no
sharing, and swallowing any children with even the most remote
chance of unseating Kronos. As it insisted to the FCC in 1968,
competition was inconsistent with its very mission of running
a phone system: hence the Bell companies "must have absolute
control over the quality, installation, and maintenance of all
parts of the [telephone] system in order effectively to carry out
that responsibility." Much trouble came from this deep aver-
sion to competition. Almost as if unable to help itself, it did
everything it could to kill MCI, a tiny rival that used microwave
towers to offer cheaper long distance services. Over the 1970s,
like an enraged bull, the firm became even more aggressive in its
attacks on competitors, despite the ongoing investigation. Its
seventh decade would be its last.

In addition to the economic, there were particular political, even Constitutional, justifications for the AT&T lawsuit.
As a regulated monopolist, AT&T had a resistance to competitors born of government support. Congress had, at times, made
it illegal to compete with AT&T in some markets. And at times
the FCC had been willing to assist the monopolist in its exter-
mination of even relatively minor competitors, like those who
sought to attach "foreign" equipment (like answering machines)
to the phone lines. In short, given both the firm's entrenchment
and its relationship with government, expecting "the market" to
naturally limit the firm's monopoly was wishful thinking.

One of the real triggers for the Justice Department, however, was signs that AT&T was also resistant even to government control. Over the 1970s, the FCC, in a change of policy,
was actually trying to introduce competition in equipment and
long-distance services. In a particularly farsighted effort, the

FCC introduced an ancestor to Net Neutrality rules, in an effort to protect the first "online service providers" from death or destruction by the monopolist. But Bell managed to subvert or undermine many of these policies, thwarting the introduction of competition, running roughshod over the FCC. As in Theodore Roosevelt's time, the idea of a monopolist that considered itself above government control compelled the Justice Department to action.

The AT&T litigation lasted a decade, but created no great court decision, and in fact the Supreme Court never weighed in. Instead, in the early 1980s, during the Reagan administration, AT&T agreed to a dramatic breakup that echoed those of the classic trusts. The firm held on to its long distance services, Bell Labs, and Western Electric, its equipment manufacturer. But seven separate regional operating companies would be carved from the corporate carcass, the local monopolists now released as independent companies. Since each of the so-called Baby Bells would continue to have an effective monopoly over local services, each was placed in a newly designed regulatory cage of reinforced and toughened FCC rules. Each would be obliged to accept connections from any long distance company (not just their former parent), and all were explicitly shut out of new markets such as online services and cable.

As the last major breakup, it is worth examining what consequence it had. It unquestionably created chaos over the short term. Some economists point to lower prices in the wake of the dissolution, but the real impact was different and far more important. It became apparent, in retrospect, just how much innovation the Bell system monopoly had been holding back. For out of the carcass of AT&T emerged entirely new types of industries unimagined or unimaginable during the reign of AT&T. For example, the liberty to sell things to consumers that plugged into a (new) phone jack not only yielded the answering machine, but the home modulator/demodulator, or modem, allowing a home computer to speak with a network. That, in turn, made feasible an industry of "online service providers" like AOL or Compuserve, which themselves spawned internet service providers that were accessible from home, producing the Internet revolution.

Politically, the slicing and dicing of the Bell System weakened the political power wielded by the entity, and made it harder to control or destroy the entrants into mobile phone service like T-Mobile and Sprint. For a while, over the 1990s, the split between AT&T (in long distance) and the underlying Bell companies created some equality of arms in the world of telecommunications lobbying, lasting at least until the Bush administration foolishly allowed the Bell system to reconsolidate into two large empires.

Obviously not everything that happened over the 1980s and 1990s can be attributed to the AT&T breakup, but so many of the basics were impossible under the Bell system that real credit must be given. We might also consider nations that did not break up their telephone monopolies. The Europeans, always more corporatist, left their telecom monopolists intact, and found their computing industries perpetually relegated to the sidelines. But perhaps the strongest counterexample is Japan, which, by the 1980s, was considered a serious rival to the United States in technology industries such as computing and online services. But because Japan never broke the power of its telephone monopoly, independent telecommunications

98 and internet firms never really grew, and by the early 2000s the United States had leaped far ahead. There is, after all, only so much you can do when your innovations need to be engineered not to disturb the mother ship.

Microsoft

Joel Klein was President Bill Clinton's second head of antitrust at the Justice Department, and many thought Klein would a mild-mannered *laissez-faire* kind of guy. But he surprised everyone by seizing the mantle of the Trustbuster to prosecute the last of the big cases of the twentieth century, against the Microsoft monopoly. "Where I think there is a case, I want to litigate," he told the *Washington Post*. "I'm not looking for seven cents on the dollar, or something like that."

Microsoft, in the 1990s, was a different sort of creature than the gentler giant it would later become. It was an aggressive, cunning, and often abusive machine, ruthless in its dispatch of its various rivals. Its founder and leader, Bill Gates, before he became a philanthropist, was the archetype of the evil nerd, a brilliant strategist who, while rarely holding the better technologies, nonetheless managed to consistently beat and outplay firms that did.

Gates had an undeniable gift for foreseeing the future and the ambition to try to always control it. By 1995, he'd noticed that this whole "internet" thing might threaten Microsoft's dominance over much of the computing industries. As he pointed out in a secret memo entitled "The Internet tidal wave," it was very possible that people might come to think of the web as more important than the applications running on their computers, and of the browser as more important than their operating systems. He was right: Microsoft's two main monopolies were endangered.

Gates also had an acute sensitivity to where the points of control in his industry were to be found: He quickly seized on the browser as the key to the future. At the time, the leading browser was a darling little company named Netscape, whose Navigator was the first browser of truly mass popularity. To control the browser, Gates realized, was to gain control over the future of the web, and, as it later became clear, pretty much the future of the world.

It was an acute insight, but not an unfamiliar one, because it was actually a replica of the maneuver that Gates had built his entire fortune on. From the beginning, Microsoft had proven the mantra that good artists copy but great artists steal. Its first operating system (MS-DOS) was actually a clone of CP/M, another operating system.* Microsoft Windows was a rip-off of the Apple Macintosh operating system; Microsoft Word and Excel were copies of Wordperfect and Lotus 1-2-3, respectively. In no instance were Microsoft's products actually better in a clear way—instead, they were always bundled with something else you really needed. Microsoft's products never won by choice, but rather, by the sense that there was no real choice.

By the late 1990s Microsoft had unleashed its signature strategy against Netscape. Explorer was Microsoft's copy of Navigator, and suddenly Explorer was everywhere and Navigator nowhere. That was no accident, but rather the byproduct

---

*The core of MS-DOS, moreover, was acquired from another firm, Seattle Computer Products.

of coercive deals pushed by Microsoft on the entire industry. In a few short years, Netscape was bankrupt, and Microsoft had added a new monopoly to its collection.

In our times, with minimal antitrust enforcement, Microsoft would have been in a perfect position to control the future of the internet, just as Gates had planned. Small firms like Google, Facebook, Amazon, and others were all dependent on the web browser, over which Microsoft now had a monopoly. To take just one example, it is highly doubtful that Google would have achieved dominance in a world where Microsoft could dictate what search engine was being used on every computer in the world. We would all be using BING.

Microsoft was a monopolist with over 90 percent of the market share, engaged in the destruction of a small company with the goal of acquiring a new monopoly in a new market. Nonetheless, the critics of antitrust attacked Klein for bringing suit. Tech markets were too complicated or "fast-moving" for the law to catch up and understand. The government would kill the goose that lays the golden egg.

But the facts, as they came out, strongly favored the Justice Department. Microsoft's motives were made clear by its internal memoranda; and Microsoft had great difficult coming up with anything but the most pretextual reasons for the tactics it employed against Netscape. Bill Gates endured a brutal and lengthy deposition, which, if it did not score any fatal blows, revealed a far darker side to the man than his various hagiographies had depicted.

The Justice Department won in district court, and then won on appeal, and seemed to be cruising toward another big breakup. "Big case" antitrust, it seemed, was alive and well. But it was just about then that George W. Bush won the 2000 presidential election, by a small and contested margin of the Florida vote. Not too long thereafter, his Justice Department decided to settle the Microsoft litigation, instead of seeking the traditional breakup. It was a sign of things to come, for with that, the campaigns against monopoly and overconcentration were about to enter their deepest freeze since the time of William McKinley.

Chicago Triumphant

If the public now knows the name Robert Bork, it is for his failure to become confirmed to the Supreme Court in the 1980s, yielding the verb "to Bork" a candidate. But in retrospect his ideas proved far more influential than most of the justices whom he failed to join. By the early 2000s, antitrust was not merely pruned but enfeebled, with most of antitrust's anti-concentration agenda wiped out. In many areas, but especially the laws governing bigness, concentration, and monopoly, the law was severely weakened, and in some cases, completely abandoned.

How did it happen? We have said that Bork was, above all, a great lawyer; the Chicago School's success came mainly through the courts, where antitrust became attached to a broader backlash against 1960s and 1970s judicial activism.

At first, in the late 1970s the Chicago-driven attack was at the margins of the antitrust law's war on monopoly, concentrated on the subject of "vertical restraints," the complex rules by which producers deal with their retailers. During peak

antitrust, in the late 1960s, the Supreme Court had imposed an   103
absolute ban on nearly all such limits, regardless of their rationale. That absolute ban was difficult to defend, and was the first
to collapse.

But it was in these cases, over which reasonable minds
could disagree, that antitrust lost its traditional goals. The
Supreme Court, in these cases, almost casually abandoned the
foundation of the law, adopting Bork's theory that the end goal
of the antitrust laws was nothing more than the "protection of
consumer welfare." The symbolic capstone was a 1979 line in an
opinion by Chief Justice Burger writing that "Congress designed
the Sherman Act as a 'consumer welfare prescription.'" His citation: "R. Bork, The Antitrust Paradox 66 (1979)."

It is, however, unfair to give Chicago all the credit, because
its theories began to gain intellectual and academic influence in
what could be described as a case of good intentions gone awry.
By the 1970s, if Chicago represented a fringe of intellectual
thought, the center was occupied by the Harvard School, and in
particular, by two professors, Donald Turner and Philip Areeda,
the authors of what remains the most influential guide to the
antitrust laws. Turner had been head of the Justice Department's Antitrust division in the late 1960s, the first lawyer who
was also a PhD economist to hold that role. He was determined
to bring greater intellectual and economic rigor to what the
department was doing. Both Turner and Areeda were sensitive
to the critique that antitrust had become the province of "coon-
skin cap" law enforcement—the blind firing of muskets at companies that just seemed bad.

Nor were these criticisms baseless. While vigorously en-
forcing the new 1950 anti-merger law, lawyers in the Kennedy

and Johnson administrations had grown aggressive, and blocked some relatively minor mergers, as in the famous *Von's Grocery* case, where the Justice Department undid a merger between two Los Angeles grocery chains with a combined market share of merely 7.5 percent. In its defense, the Justice Department maintained that Congress was concerned about "creeping" concentration, achieved "not in a single acquisition but as the result of a series of acquisitions." But it can still be asked whether merger actually inhibited competition in any meaningful way. It gave grounds to Bork's charge that law enforcement in the 1960s was out of control—the Justice Department was like the "sheriff of a frontier town: he did not sift evidence, distinguish between suspects, and solve crimes, but merely walked the main street and every so often pistol-whipped a few people."

Turner was, on the one hand, not shy to use the power of government. He believed, for example, that longstanding monopolies should be just broken up, regardless of whether they had done anything "wrong" or were a "bad trust." As Turner's deputy and future Nobel laureate Oliver Williamson put it, "[The] persistent dominance of an industry by a single firm is not to be expected," and long-term, sustained dominance "should be regarded as an actionable manifestation of market failure."

But Turner was also intensely devoted to increasing the influence of economics over antitrust law and enforcement, and he and Areeda increasingly accepted the premise that greater rigor meant an acceptance of the narrower theory of harm, suggested by price theory—in other words, the consumer welfare standard. To be sure, as authors of a guide to the law, the men were bound to report on the law as it existed, meaning that

Turner and Areeda were bound to accept the Supreme Court's adoption of Chicago's main premises. But there was more to it than this—there was a defensiveness born out of a decade of stinging attacks by some of Chicago's most brilliant economists and lawyers. And so without any grand declaration, it was the Harvard School that quietly made mainstream the premise that "consumer welfare" should be the measure of all things antitrust.

In this way, Bork won the culture war, by convincing a vast middle comprising practicing lawyers and judges seeking respectability with the appearance of rigor. If Bork himself could be too spicy and even a little bit frightening, Turner and Areeda served up the blander, more reassuring fare favored by judges and practicing attorneys. As Rebecca Allensworth writes, the Harvard School "grafted economic thinking onto existing antitrust doctrine in a way that was both more moderate and more workable" than Chicago, but accepting of its main premises. Bit by bit, the Chicago critique reached deeper into antitrust law—zooming past the matter of vertical restraints and reaching the historic core of the law: the problem of monopoly. And here, breaking with its primary mandate, antitrust law underwent a truly radical change and suddenly became extraordinarily tolerant of the monopolist's conduct.

Let us dwell for a moment on this. It is true that the original Trust Movement, and men like John D. Rockefeller, had argued that monopoly was inherently efficient and spiritually uplifting. But by the 1980s, monopoly was out of fashion, and competition was as American as apple pie. Some other approach was needed, and indeed was developed during the AT&T and IBM trials over the 1970s. It was during the defense of IBM and

AT&T that the Chicago School and the opponents of antitrust finally found ways to stop worrying and fall in love with the monopoly form.

The contemporary monopolist, it turned out, had been gravely misunderstood. He was not the threatening brute feared by previous generations, but a well-meaning and timid creature, almost a gentle giant, whose every action was well-intentioned, and who lived in constant fear of new competitors. Even if he had already killed his actual competitors, he was nonetheless restrained, by just the thought of them. For that reason, he would not dare raise prices or destroy his rivals.* This theory was deployed to defend AT&T, among the most entrenched monopolists in American history, yet apparently so afraid of potential competition that any wrongdoing was unthinkable.†

When it came to the monopolist's conduct, both antitrust enforcers and Congress were guilty of a similar misunderstanding. What Congress had condemned as abusive conduct—predatory pricing, price discrimination, coercive tying of unwanted products—was really no such thing, but being practiced for the best and happiest of reasons. A cascade of Chicago School papers based purely on pricing theory and ignoring any strategic considerations (let alone evidence), suggested that the monopolist had little to gain from these practices, and so

---

*The premise that elevated prices alone might attract new competitors is not irrational; yet where the premise falls short is ignoring the fact that exclusionary tactics, the concern of the Sherman Act, might well keep out potential competitors while also allowing collection of higher profits.

†Economist William Baumol is most associated with the theory of "contestable markets" alluded to here, but by that phrase he meant markets where entry is costless and exit free, which was decidedly not the case for AT&T.

must presumably be doing them to make their operations more efficient. After all, as McGee had said, one must always presume that "the existing structure is the efficient structure."

Jumping from theory to reality in a novel way, the Chicago School then asserted that that which did not exist in theory probably did not exist in practice. Robbing banks is economically irrational, given security guards and meager returns; *ergo* bank robbing does not happen; *ergo* there is no need for the criminal law. Exaggerated only slightly, this premise has been at the core of Bork-Chicago antitrust for more than thirty years.

The absurdity of its logic and its rejection of Congressional intent is what ultimately made the movement political, even while it always strenuously avoided the claim. It didn't matter that Congress wanted many mergers blocked (the 1950 law), or wanted small businesses protected (the Robinson-Patman Act of 1936). Those laws "didn't make economic sense" and therefore could be ignored, or should only be enforced in a "sensible" way, meaning the Chicago way, Congress be damned. In this sense, economics held a trump over the plain text of the law in a manner that can only be described as Constitutional. Bork, who styled himself an opponent of "judicial activism," was perfectly happy to allow his own political and economic preferences to trump the clearly expressed will of Congress.

The Chicago movement, unsurprisingly, began to encounter major resistance during the 1980s through the 2000s. A group of economists and other academics, styled the "post-Chicago" school, emerged to challenge many of its basic premises. What the post-Chicago academics demonstrated was this: Even if you took a strictly economic view of the antitrust laws, you didn't actually reach Bork's conclusions.

On further inspection, it *did* make sense for a dominant firm to create barriers to competitors and generally "raise rivals' costs," as prominent antitrust economists Thomas Krattenmaker and Steven Salop put it. Thickets of patents were sometimes deployed to slow down those seeking to bring new products to market, said economist Carl Shapiro. Merger enforcement should take seriously dynamic effects on innovation, said Michael Katz and Howard Shelanski. Exclusion should be a core concern of the antitrust laws, wrote economist Jon Baker. Newer econometric techniques used by scholars like Daniel Rubinfeld might measure the harms that Chicago tended to assume away.

Most members of the post-Chicago school were economists who were chagrined and dismayed by the misuse of economic tools to justify a *laissez-faire* ideology that was always suspiciously in line with the dictates of big business. A new group, the American Antitrust Institute, was founded in 1998 by Albert Foer to create an institutional counterweight to antitrust erosion. And a leader of the resistance was Robert Pitofsky, who, as the FTC's chairman, restored it to fighting weight, and who asserted that "[b]ecause extreme interpretations and misinterpretations of conservative economic theory (and constant disregard of facts) have come to dominate antitrust, there is reason to believe that the United States is headed in a profoundly wrong direction."

But the Clinton years were, in the end, just a speed-bump, for during the Bush years, the anti-monopoly provisions of the Sherman Act went into a deep freeze from which they have never really recovered. After pausing briefly to settle the Microsoft case, the Bush Justice Department proceeded to bring a grand total of zero anti-monopoly antitrust cases over a period of eight years, and did not block any major mergers. The judiciary continued to drift toward Bork, and with a Supreme Court intent on cracking down on private plaintiffs using the law, antitrust wandered further and further from its origins, leaving far behind its Congressional intent.

By the second term of the Bush administration, antitrust had drifted very far from having a say about the structure of the economy, and increasingly became something that merely governed explicit price-fixing cartels, blatant mergers to monopoly, and little else. If one wanted to mark a point as the fall of Brandeisian antitrust, it would be 2004, when the Supreme Court, under Justice Antonin Scalia, elevated what was once called "the evil of monopoly" to something different: an essential motivating factor within the American economy. In an unnecessary aside, Scalia wrote:

> The mere possession of monopoly power, and the concomitant charging of monopoly prices, is not only not unlawful; it is an important element of the free-market system. The opportunity to charge monopoly prices—at least for a short period— is what attracts "business acumen" in the first place; it induces risk taking that produces innovation and economic growth.

If the Chicago School had once portrayed the monopolist as a gentle giant, he had now become something akin to an Ayn Randian hero. In the underlying case, the defendant was Verizon, who despite holding a monopoly for nearly a hundred years, was supposedly encouraging others to take risks, even as it destroyed the entrepreneurs who had actually taken the risks. This was an antitrust with the "anti" removed, a law that now glorified monopoly instead of condemning it.

In Defense of the Big Case Tradition

In the United States, there have been no trustbusting or "big cases" for nearly twenty years: no cases targeting an industry-spanning monopolist or super-monopolist, seeking the goal of breakup. As we've seen, that was the original tradition of anti-trust enforcement pioneered by Theodore Roosevelt. But in our times tradition has fallen victim to a defamation campaign. The big cases have been portrayed as wasteful and useless, and breakups, the original remedy, as too radical to take seriously. The Justice Department and the FTC have been depicted as bumblers who can't do anything right, or bullies who unfairly attacked successful firms, and in their misguided efforts, did nothing but hurt the American economy and punish winners.

It is time to rehabilitate the reputation of the big cases, give them their due, and stress their importance—particularly for a dynamic, technologically driven economy. We have already discussed the AT&T case and its dramatic reboot of the communication industries, transforming a stagnant backwater into a centerpiece of the American economy. Similarly, the Microsoft case must be given credit for preventing the giant from dominating the nascent web economy of the early 2000s. But the defense can also be made even for cases that had been widely decried as failures and seen as examples against bringing big monopoly-busting cases at all.

Exhibit A is the case against the IBM monopoly, which, next to AT&T, was the biggest antitrust case of the 1970s. IBM is today a relatively mellow, service-oriented company, but "Big Blue" was once the great monopolist of computing with a terrifying reputation. The United States sued IBM in 1969, alleging that it had illegally maintained its monopoly in general purpose computing using a variety of measures, including sabotage at the sales level and false product announcements.

The case, which lasted an extraordinary thirteen years (including six years of trial), came under extraordinary attack. It was dubbed "the antitrust division's Vietnam" by Robert Bork and a "monument to arrogance" by scholar John Lopatka. Steven Brill, the founder of *American Lawyer*, wrote a scathing attack on the IBM trial, depicting the government's lawyers as incompetent, the judge hungry to make his name, all of them feasting on a great American corporation, yet accomplishing nothing in the end. Brill called the case "a farce of such mindboggling proportions that any lawyer who now tries to find out about it . . . will be risking the same quicksand that devoured the lawyers involved in the case."

The government's battle with IBM did reach epic proportions. At the lengthy trial, the government's presentation took 104,000 pages of transcript, while for its part, IBM called 856 witnesses and cited 12,280 exhibits. In legal fees, the case consumed millions, if not hundreds of millions of dollars. And at the end of it, thirteen years later, the Reagan administration simply dropped the case, on the same day it settled with AT&T. Was it all just a waste of resources?

That's no trip to the county courthouse, and no one can defend how the court managed the litigation, which became as bloated as a 1970s muscle car. But consider the stakes: The computer and software industries were already bringing in billions in revenue, are today collectively worth many trillions of dollars, and include many of the most valuable companies on Earth. Small effects on this industry would and did have major longterm effects. It has become clear that the IBM case decisively influenced the computing industry that is now a centerpiece of the American and world economy.

First and most importantly, IBM dropped its practice of bundling (or tying) its software with hardware. That is broadly understood, even by IBM's own people, to have kickstarted the birth of an independent software industry. Second, the IBM litigation also affected the development of the personal computer industry in the late 1970s and early 1980s. The IBM PC, developed while the lawsuit was still pending, was antitrust proof: IBM went with an extremely open design and declined to buy or exert excessive control over the firms who made the components, including Intel, Seagate, and Microsoft, among others. IBM actually entered the personal computer market gingerly, and separately from its other products.

Above all, IBM spent the 1970s with a "policeman at the elbow," and subsequent research makes clear that the firm steered shy of anything close to anticompetitive conduct, for fear of adding to the case against it.* The period consequently saw the birth of independent software, the dawn of the personal computer, the rise of firms like Apple and Microsoft—all matters, by any count, of major economic importance and of great value to the American economy.

How much the "policeman at the elbow" contributed to the extraordinary developments in the computing industry is hard to measure precisely, but if the answer is even a little bit, then the case mattered a lot. And that is why I think the whining

* A much deeper dive into the IBM case can be found in Tim Wu, "Tech Dominance and the Policeman at the Elbow," forthcoming in *After the Digital Tornado* (Kevin Werbach, ed., 2019).

about the number of pages in the IBM trial record is petty, or the hassle experienced by IBM's lawyers, or the millions in costs, when hundreds of billions if not trillions were at stake. If the effect of the litigation was to prevent IBM from killing its main emergent challengers, the IBM case was not expensive, but incredibly cheap.

We have said that some have criticized the big cases because they last too long and waste too many resources. But a different critique suggests the big cases were unnecessary because the market would have reintroduced competition anyhow. This line of argument—a version of the "best of all possible worlds"— strikes me as baffling. Consider that AT&T, for example, ruled its industry for decades, destroying myriad would-be challengers, with the tacit or sometimes active assistance of government. Having waited for several decades, are society and the economy supposed to wait for several more? This line of argument ignores the idea that deliberate investments in building barriers to entry can be effective, and it is often utterly rational for the monopolist to make such investments. Of the great mysteries of the Chicago School was the fact that it posited ultra-rational, profit-seeking monopolists, yet somehow imagined that they would generally leave themselves completely vulnerable to competitive attack. The truth is that investments in barriers to entry are a magnificent investment.

It would be crazy, however, to defend every case that was brought as part of the big case tradition. For example, in the 1970s, the Federal Trade Commission went after the cereal industry based on the observation that it was profitable and somewhat concentrated. This was, challengingly, not a case about an abusive or even persistent monopoly, but rather an

114   oligopoly of about four firms. The agency believed that product differentiation (that is, products aimed at children, older people, the health-conscious, and so on) was the anti-competitive tool of choice. To even describe the theory is to reveal its absurdity.

But there is a different critique of the big case tradition that I take seriously: that it is simply much less effective than it could be, being subject to the inherent randomness of litigation. As William Kovacic, former FTC chair, once wrote, "trustbusting is the Sherman Act's most alluring and enduring mirage." As he explained, "federal enforcement officials have mounted memorable campaigns to disassemble leviathans of American business, yet the tantalizing goal of improving the economic and political order by restructuring dominant firms frequently has eluded its pursuers."

That's why some have pushed different approaches: One is the writing of pro-competitive rules for persistently uncompetitive industries. Another new law targets longstanding monopolies based on their persistence alone. The United Kingdom has such a law, known as a "Market Investigation Authority." Donald Turner of Harvard proposed a law that would create an authority to break up monopolies that had been proven to be "substantial" and "persistent" and lasted at least ten years. As he wrote, "the evils of Monopoly are largely independent of the manner in which it is achieved or maintained."

The Age of Oligopoly

We can see that it is to the George W. Bush era that we owe our present economic state, as the administration dismantled most of the checks on industry concentration. In a run that

lasted some two decades, American industry reached levels of
industry concentration arguably unseen since the original Trust
era. A full 75 percent of industries witnessed increased concentration from the years 1997 to 2012, according to an extensive
study by economist Gustavo Grullon and his co-authors, which
was echoed by studies by the Council of Economic Advisors in
the White House, and an independent study by the *Economist*
magazine.

But to get a sense beyond the statistics it is worth consid-
ering some concrete examples:

- *The AT&T monopoly*, which had been forced to divide into
  8 pieces, was allowed, over the 2000s, to reconstitute itself
  in two giant firms: Verizon and AT&T. Later, AT&T bought
  DirecTV and then TimeWarner to return close to its size in
  the 1980s. The idea of allowing AT&T to come back in such
  a fashion might have seemed shocking to those who thought
  the breakup was important to competition.
- *The airline industry*, which had been deregulated in the 1970s
  with the goal of increasing competition, was allowed to
  merge into an increasingly smaller number of "major" airlines. Delta bought Northwestern airlines; United bought
  Continental, and American bought U.S. Airlines, reducing
  the total number of traditional major airlines to just three.
  Since then, the airlines have found it easy to cooperate on
  matters like the shrinking of seats or the introduction of new
  fees, yielding unprecedented profit for years on end.
- *The cable industry*, which at one point in the 1960s had been
  an upstart challenger to the broadcasters, was allowed to

116   combine into just three major regional monopolies, facing limited competition in each area. Cable was also freed to charge monopoly prices, and happily raised monthly prices at some eight times the rate of inflation. During a period of historically low inflation, it managed to raise its prices by an impressive 8 percent per year. Bills that were once in the $30–40 range rose over $100, and as much as $200 per month.

- *The pharmaceutical industry*, which had been fairly fragmented, underwent a major consolidation from 2005 through 2017, with thousands of combinations that reduced the international market from some sixty-odd firms to about ten. This consolidation was international in scope. Meanwhile, within the United States, enforcement agencies allowed passage of a new and disturbing kind of drug acquisition: the sale of a drug to a firm whose immediate design was to take full advantage of the monopoly pricing potential, by raising prices by at least 1,000 percent and sometimes as much as 6,000 percent. The most famous example was that of an opportunistic young man named Martin Shkreli who managed to acquire the facilities for the production of a rare drug named Daraprim, and immediately increased the price from $13.50 a pill to $750. But that was just one of many similar transactions—none of which were challenged—and indeed the price of Daraprim remains at $750.

- *Ticketmaster*, the nation's dominant seller of tickets to live events, was allowed to merge with LiveNation, the nation's near-monopoly promoter of events. Among other effects, this deal allowed Ticketmaster to survive any potential

challenge in primary ticket sales stemming either from Live-
Nation's own entry, or from any internet startups.

- *Bayer,* the German descendent of the I.G. Farben monopoly, was allowed to buy Monsanto to reduce the global seed and pesticide industry to just three major players. (Other mergers include a Dow-DuPont merger and ChemChina's acquisition of Syngenta.) Over recent years, the price of a bag of seed corn has risen from $80 to $300, based on reduced competition.

- *The global beer industry* consolidated into a single firm in 2016, as Anheuser-Busch InBev and SABMiller merged. The combination controls over 2,000 beers, including most of the major non-craft brands in the world like Budweiser, Beck's Bass, Labatt's, Michelob, Corona, and Stella Artois. In the United States, Anheuser-Busch InBev and Miller-Coors control over 70 percent of beer sales.

Many of these combinations happened during the Obama administration. President Barack Obama said in 2008 that he wanted "an antitrust division in the Justice Department that actually believes in antitrust law." He appointed officials who were understood to be more enforcement-oriented. Yet when it came time to bring cases, the government faced a judiciary that had now widely accepted the Chicago and Harvard schools' premises, and enforcers often felt powerless to stop the ongoing concentration. But it would be unfair to say that all of the resistance was judicial. For among the lawyers and economists who staff the agencies, Chicago and Harvard's influence had been strongly felt. Bork's insinuation that strict reliance on economic analysis was a mark of good character had became something of a controlling meme. Those demanding a return to the law's traditions of trustbusting and breakups were cast as wild-eyed radicals in an administration that favored moderation and composure.

And of all of the blind spots during the last decade, the greatest was surely that which allowed the almost entirely uninhibited consolidation of the tech industry into a new class of monopolists.

The Rise of the Tech Trusts

Once upon a time, in the 1990s and 2000s, the web and the internet were new and everything was going to be different forever. The web formed its own special exception, not just to the laws of business but to just about everything humanity had faced before. For personal relationships, private identity, and communication styles were all different "in cyberspace." Logically, this also suggested the demise of the usual principles of business and economics.

What else could one conclude when, in the 2000s, a tiny blog could outdo an established media outlet? When startups seemed to come from nowhere, gain millions of users overnight, and make their founders and employees wealthier than the old school tycoons? The man who described the mood was author John Perry Barlow, who in the 1990s implored those interested in cyberspace to "imagine a place where trespassers leave no footprints, where goods can be stolen an infinite number of times and yet remain in the possession of their original owners, where businesses you never heard of can own the history of your personal affairs, where only children feel completely at home, where the physics is that of thought rather than things, and where everyone is as virtual as the shadows in Plato's cave."

Everything was fast and chaotic; no position was lasting. One day, AOL was dominant and all-powerful; the next, it was the subject of business books laughing at its many failures. Netscape rose and fell like a rocket that failed to achieve orbit (though Microsoft had something to do with that). MySpace, the social media pioneer, was everywhere and then nowhere. Search engines and social media sites seemed to come and go: Altavista, Bigfoot, and Friendster were household names one moment and gone the next.

The chaos made it easy to think that bigness—the economics of scale—no longer really mattered in the new economy. If anything, it seemed that being big, like being old, was just a disadvantage. Being big meant being hierarchical, industrial, dinosaurlike in an age of fleet-footed mammals. Better maybe to stay small and stay young, to move fast and break things.

All this suggested that in cyberspace, there could be no such thing as a lasting monopoly. The internet would never stand for it. Business was now moving at internet speed: A three-year-old firm was middle-aged; a five-year-old firm almost certainly near death. "Barriers to entry" was a twentieth century concept. Now, competition was always just "one click away."

Even if a firm did manage to gain temporary dominance, there was nothing to be afraid of. We were not speaking of the evil monopolists of old. The new firms were instead devoted to spreading sweetness and light, goodwill toward all men— whether access to information (Google), good books for cheap (Amazon), or the building of a global community (Facebook).

Not only did they not charge high prices, sometimes they didn't even charge at all. Google would give you free email, free map apps, free cloud storage. Hence businesses like Facebook or Google needed to be seen as more akin to a charity. Who would sue the Red Cross for its "monopoly" on disaster relief?

In these heady times, only a malcontent would dare suggest that just maybe, business and economics had not quite been reinvented forever. Or that what was taken to be a new order might, in fact, just be a phase that was destined to come to an end as firms better understood the market and its new technologies. The good times were on.

After a decade of open chaos and easy market entry, something surprising did happen. A few firms—Google, Ebay, Facebook, and Amazon—did not disappear. They hit that five-year mark of obsolescence with no signs of impending collapse or retirement. Instead, the major firms seemed to be sticking, and even growing in their dominance. Suddenly, there weren't a dozen search engines, each with a different idea, but one search engine. There were no longer hundreds of stores that everyone went to, but one "everything store." And to avoid Facebook was to make yourself a digital hermit. There stopped being a next new thing, or at least, a new thing that was a serious challenge to the old thing.

Unfortunately, antitrust law failed to notice that the 1990s were over. Instead, for a decade and counting, it gave the major tech players a pass—even when confronting fairly obvious dangers and anticompetitive mergers. That is best exemplified by the Facebook story.

Launched in 2004, Facebook quickly dispatched its rival MySpace, which had been a rare Los Angeles tech success story, but had become a mess of intrusive advertising, fake users, and trolls. In just a few years, Facebook achieved an early dominance over general purpose social networking.

But by the 2010s, Facebook faced one of its most serious challengers, a startup named Instagram. Instagram combined a camera app with a social network on which it was easy and fast to share photos on mobile. It was popular with younger people, and it was not long before some of its advantages over Facebook were noticed. As business writer Nicholas Carlson said at the time, Instagram "allows people to do what they like to do on Facebook easier and faster."

Having already gained 30 million users in just eighteen months of existence, Instagram was poised to become a leading challenger to Facebook based on its strength on mobile platforms, where Facebook was weak. By the doctrine of internet time, Facebook, then eight years old, was supposed to be heading into retirement.

But the disruption narrative was rudely interrupted. Instead of surrendering to the inevitable, Facebook realized it could just buy out the new. For just $1 billion, Facebook eliminated its existential problem and reassured its investors. As *TIME* would put it, "Buying Instagram conveyed to investors that the company was serious about dominating the mobile ecosystem while also neutralizing a nascent competitor."

When a dominant firm buys its a nascent challenger, alarm bells are supposed to ring. Yet both American and European regulators found themselves unable to find anything wrong with the takeover. The American analysis remains secret, but we have the United Kingdom's report. Its analysis, such as it was, went as follows. Facebook did not have an important photo-taking app, meaning that Facebook was not competing with Instagram for consumers. Instagram did not have advertising revenue, so it did not compete with Facebook either. Hence, the report was able to reach the extraordinary conclusion that Facebook and Instagram were not competitors.

It takes many years of training to reach conclusions this absurd. A teenager could have told you that Facebook and Instagram were competitors—after all, teenagers were the ones who were switching platforms. With this level of insight, the world's governments in the 2010s did nothing to stop the largest firms from buying everyone and anyone who might be a potential threat, in a buying spree worthy of John D. Rockefeller himself. Nothing was learned from the Instagram failure: Facebook was able to buy its next greatest challenger, WhatsApp, which offered a more privacy-protective and messaging-centered competitive threat. The $19 billion buyout—as suspicious as J.P. Morgan's bribe of Andrew Carnegie—somehow failed to raise any alarm. At the time, many were shocked at the price. But when one is actually agreeing to split a monopoly as lucrative as generalized social media, with over $50 billion in annual revenue, the price suddenly makes sense.

In total, Facebook managed to string together 67 unchallenged acquisitions, which seems impressive, unless you consider that Amazon undertook 91 and Google got away with 214 (a few of which were conditioned). In this way, the tech industry became essentially composed of just a few giant trusts: Google for search and related industries, Facebook for social media, Amazon for online commerce. While competitors remained in the wings, their positions became marginalized with every passing day.

If many of these acquisition were small, or mere "acqui-hires" (i.e., acquisitions to hire employees), others, like Facebook's takeover of Instagram and Whatsapp, eliminated serious competitive threats. In the 2000s, Google had launched "Google Video" and done pretty well, but not compared to its greatest competitor, YouTube. Google bought YouTube without a peep from the competition agencies. Waze, an upstart online mapping company, was poised to be an on-ramp for Google's vertical challengers, until Google, the owner of its own dominant online mapping program, bought the firm in a fairly blatant merger to monopoly. Google also acquired AdMob, its most serious competitor for online advertising, which the government let happen on the premise that Apple might also enter the market in a serious way (they didn't). Amazon acquired would-be competitors like Zappos, Diapers.com, and Soap.com.

These were hardly coercive takeovers, as practiced by Standard Oil. Most of these firms were happy to have a big fat buyout. But if the takeovers were friendlier, their net effect was little different than John D. Rockefeller's campaign: the continued domination by the trusts. This was obvious to the business press. As *Techcrunch* opined of the 2014 WhatsApp acquisition, "Facebook [now] possesses the most popular messaging app, and has neutralized the biggest threat to its global domination of social networking." Or as another business analyst wrote at the time: "Without this acquisition, 'uncool' Facebook would have been in a very difficult competitive position against its cooler messaging apps rivals [which] would have posed an existential threat for Facebook. By acquiring the leader in messaging apps, Facebook has removed this threat."

Where buyouts were not practical, the tech firms tried a different approach: "cloning," the favorite tactic of Microsoft back in the day. Faced with potential competitive challenge from Yelp's popular reviews of local businesses in the early 2010s, Google created its own "local" sites attached to Google maps. The value in any such site would rest in the quality of its user reviews, and as a newcomer, Google didn't have any of those. It solved the problem by simply purloining Yelp's reviews and putting them on its site, making Yelp essentially redundant, and also harvesting the proceeds of its many years of work.*

Meanwhile, Facebook cloned so many of its rival Snapchat's features that it began to seem like a running joke. Amazon has a track record of cloning products that succeed so it can help itself to the margins. To be sure, there is nothing wrong with firms copying to learn from each other; that's how innovation can happen. But there is a line where copying and exclusion becomes anti-competitive, where the goal becomes the maintenance of monopoly as opposed to real improvement. When Facebook spies on competitors, or summons a firm to a meeting just to figure out how to copy it more accurately, or discourages funding of competitors, a line is crossed.

Over the years, as with the original Trust Movement, a strong current of self-justification began to creep into the consolidation. This could be a somewhat awkward undertaking for some of the firms who, as startups, had been committed to the

*The FTC, in the course of an investigation, told Google to knock it off, and Google grudgingly stopped taking Yelp's reviews, though it insisted it was doing Yelp a favor. It nonetheless maintained its Yelp clones, and, in the style of Microsoft, did everything it could to make its own local results show up, even though they were inferior by Google's own metrics.

old internet ideals of openness and chaos. But now it was all for the best: a law of nature, a chance for the monopolists to do good for the universe. The cheerer-in-chief for the monopoly form is Peter Thiel, author of *Competition Is for Losers*. Labeling the competitive economy a "relic of history" and a "trap," he proclaimed that "only one thing can allow a business to transcend the daily brute struggle for survival: monopoly profits."

The big tech firms are a little more circumspect than Thiel. For Facebook, it is not trying to build a global empire of influence so much as "bringing the world closer together." It is supposedly a "different kind of company that connects billions of people." To do that right, however, requires a global monopoly. Meanwhile, Google wants to organize the world's information, but to do so they need to get their hands on all the information in the world. Amazon, meanwhile, wants nothing more than to serve the consumer, which is great, and you can check out any time you like, but you can never leave.

If there is a sector more ripe for the reinvigoration of the big case tradition, I do not know it.

A Neo-Brandeisian Agenda

Some effort to revive the antitrust laws may be an inevitability in a nation founded on principles of anti-monopoly, equality, and decentralized power. What should be done? It's not enough to demand change without providing an agenda that enjoys legal legitimacy, can make use of the best economic tools, and is usable by enforcers, judges, and industry itself. That is the aspiration of this last section.

1. Merger Review

The priority for Neo-Brandeisian antitrust is the reform of merger review. Rereading the legislative history of the Anti-Merger Act of 1950, one is struck by how far current practice has drifted from what Congress intended. As the Supreme Court put it, the law sought to erect "a barrier to what Congress saw was the rising tide of economic concentration" and therefore provided "authority for arresting mergers at a time when the trend to a lessening of competition in a line of commerce was

128   still in its incipiency." For "Congress saw the process of concentration in American business as a dynamic force" and it wanted
to give the government and courts "the power to brake this force
at its outset and before it gathered momentum."

Merger control has wandered so far from Congress's expressed intent in 1950 as to make a mockery of the democratic
process. Congress instructed the courts to block a merger when
its effect "may be substantially to lessen competition." Yet
somehow, as in other areas, the agencies have read into this language something that is obviously not in the text of the law: a
general requirement that clear proof of higher prices after the
merger be provided. This has made every merger battle into a
highly technical battle of experts having little to do with the
original concerns of the law. Consider, for example, the 2018
merger between AT&T and TimeWarner—the kind of merger
the law clearly intended to block—which in practice came to turn
on a technical wrangling over whether cable customers might
end up paying an extra 45 cents per month for their TV service.

Even within a purely economic framework, merger review
is flawed. The fact that a merger may be designed to eliminate a
future or "potential" competitor is often ignored as too speculative. That's why American and European agencies allowed
Facebook and Google to buy many of their major potential competitors. Innovation and dynamic effects, being harder to measure, do not get due consideration.

To abandon economic analysis entirely would be implau-
sible. But what's needed are broader and tougher merger standards, especially when it comes to the largest, most important
mergers. This is an area where legislative action is warranted

to make clear, at a minimum, that the Anti-Merger Act of 1950 meant what it said. Here is not the right place for a full discussion of reforms, but they might at a minimum include setting a higher bar for giant mergers (over $6 billion in value). The problem of overlapping ownership of horizontal rivals highlighted by Professor Einer Elhauge should be addressed, and we might also consider a return to structural presumptions, such as a simple but *per se* ban on mergers that reduce the number of major firms to less than four.* Whatever the proposals may be, an overhaul of merger review is a priority.

2. Democratization of the Merger Process

Since the Trust era, giant mergers have been of great concern to the public, implicating consolidation, inequality, and the very state of capitalism itself. Nonetheless, with rare exceptions, there is today limited public debate over actual mergers. One explanation is that economic policy is complex, and that Americans are interested in other, more entertaining parts of politics. But another reason is the incredibly secretive and technical nature of the process, which particularly contributes to the decision not to challenge a merger. Even the Supreme Court and the Federal Reserve have greater openness in their proceedings. It is hard for the public or the press to care without any opportunity to know what is going on.

*In today's economy, many natural competitors, like the major U.S. airlines, have the same institutional owners, which may facilitate cooperation instead of competition. See Azar, José and Schmalz, Martin C. and Tecu, Isabel, "Anticompetitive Effects of Common Ownership," *Journal of Finance* 73(4), May 10, 2018.

The problem is path dependent, for mergers have fallen between agency and judicial process, and live in their own realm. Judicial process, while in some tension with democratic principles, is part of the Constitutional system, and has numerous traditional safeguards. Judges are appointed and confirmed, the proceedings are public, and the decisions are explained.

In contemporary practice, however, the prior agency review has become the de facto process of importance in nearly all cases. And, drawing on prosecutorial, as opposed to judicial or administrative norms, it is a secret process with extensive rules designed to protect all involved, as in criminal investigation. But everyone knows the merger is being reviewed, and one can usually guess who is involved and what is being said. It is unclear whether the values being served by the secrecy are worth the cost.

One remedy is to recognize that merger review is a quasi-judicial, administrative process, and one that the public deserves to know more about. Industry comments on a major merger should be filed publicly, not in secret, and any interested member of the public should be encouraged to file comments. Finally, in major mergers, the agency, if it plans on a consent agreement, should put out its proposed remedy for meaningful public comment.

For merger reviews are too important to the public to be so secret. Some might suggest the result would be politicization of merger review—but big mergers *are* political, and the idea that the public or its representatives be kept in the dark is hard to support. The suggested reforms would reopen the tradition of spirited public debate over major mergers, as opposed to the stealthy consolidation of industries that is today's reality.

3. Big Cases   131

The phrase "trustbuster" dates to the turn of the twentieth century, and as we've said, it is here that antitrust law owes its debt to President Theodore Roosevelt. Tradition and norms of enforcement can matter as much, if not more, than what the law says. Through the 1970s and even into the 1990s, attacks on persistent monopoly remained a mainstay of antitrust enforcement practice, particularly at the Justice Department. That tradition, one that's at the core of the Sherman Act, has been lost. The last major Section 2 case seeking dissolution of an industrywide firm was the Microsoft trial; the last major breakup was the AT&T litigation.

Attacks on the trusts will always encounter resistance, not least from the target itself. But little could be closer to obeying Congressional intent than to use the Sherman Act against the trusts, or monopolies, of the era. It is here, among other places, that America can borrow from Europe, which has never given up on the big cases, and continues to enforce a law it borrowed from the United States in a manner more like America once did. Europe now leads in the scrutiny of "big tech," including the case against Google's practices, and in smaller, less public matters, like policing how Apple deals with competitors who also depend on the iPhone platform. European antitrust is far from perfect, but its leadership and willingness to bring big cases when competition is clearly under threat should serve as a model for American enforcers and for the rest of the world.

4. Breakups

Breakups and the blocking of mergers (also known as "structural relief") are at the historic core of the antitrust program, and should not be shied away from unduly. Breakups, done right, have clear effects. They can completely realign an industry's incentives, and can, at their best, transform a stagnant industry into a dynamic one.

There is an unfortunate tendency within enforcement agencies to portray breakups and dissolutions as off the table or only for extremely rare cases. There is no legal reason for that presumption: Indeed, the original practice favored dissolution as the default remedy—implied in the very word "antitrust."

Too much of the resistance to dissolution comes from taking too seriously the legal fiction of corporate personhood. In reality, a large corporation is made up of sub-units, whether functional or regional, or independent operations that have been previously acquired. It is not "impossible" to administer a breakup as is sometimes claimed. Many breakups are akin to the spinoffs or dissolutions that are not uncommon in business practice as it stands, such as AOL-Time-Warner's decision to break itself up into multiple units in the early 2000s. While the purpose is and should be public benefit, in some cases, like Standard Oil, the breakup may actually be healthy for the firm itself, but thanks to ego, otherwise known as agency problems, something it would not do itself.

Consider a breakup of Facebook that undid the mergers with Instagram and WhatsApp. While Facebook might not like being dissolved, and might find the new competition unwelcome, it

is hard to see what the great social cost, if any, would be. It is
not clear that there are important social efficiencies gained by
the combination of these firms. But reintroducing competition
into the social media space, perhaps even quality competition,
measured by matters like greater protection of privacy, could
mean a lot to the public. And we have not even touched upon the
non-economic concerns, such as the concentration of so much
power over speech into a single platform, and the clear dangers to democracy that stem from manipulation of the Facebook
conglomerate. The simplest way to break the power of Facebook
is breaking up Facebook.

This suggestion dovetails with a more technical but
important concern over the use of consent decrees as the
main antitrust remedy. As American and European enforcers
have relied heavily on consent decrees and settlements,
their management can be overwhelming. The agencies are
resource-constrained, and their best expertise lies in investigation and enforcement, not compliance and monitoring. By the
mid-2010s, for example, the sheer number of Justice Department consent decrees covering the beer industry was vexing.
And the level of dedicated government oversight necessary
to monitor every consent decree effectively would give even
believers in government some qualms. Breakups or structural
remedies are, effectively, self-executing, and thereby a much
cleaner way of dealing with competition problems.

5. Market Investigations and Competition Rules

In 2007, the United Kingdom, using a device known as the
"market investigation," studied the conditions of competition

among airports in the London and Edinburgh regions, and concluded that the joint ownership of Heathrow, Gatwick, Stansted, and four other airports was neither necessary nor serving the public. It proposed a divestiture that left the major airports competing for business: especially Heathrow, Gatwick, and Stansted. While strenuously resisted and fought in the British courts, the results have been widely lauded, yielding higher service quality and greater efficiency by various measures.

The United States can and should adopt a market investigations law like that of the UK, and give it to the Federal Trade Commission to enforce. The prerequisite would be persistent dominance of at least ten years or longer, suggesting that a market remedy is not forthcoming, and proof that the existing industry structure lacked convincing competitive or public justifications, and that market forces would be unlikely to remedy the situation by themselves. In practice, the agency would put overly consolidated industry under investigation, recommend remedies through the administration process, and adopt them, subject to judicial review. The market investigation would serve as a particularly effective tool for stagnant and longstanding but not particularly abusive or aggressive monopolies or duopolies. The United States and Europe can both make headway employing pro-competitive rules instead of bringing cases, an approach championed both by the Obama White House and FCC Commissioner Rohit Chopra. The basic approach, which has already been used to great effect in some industries, calls for rules designed explicitly to weaken obvious barriers to market entry or otherwise promote a healthy competitive process.

6. Antitrust's Goals

There is good reason to think that antitrust's intended economic and political roles cannot be fully recovered without jettisoning the absurd and exaggerated premise that "Congress designed the Sherman Act as a 'consumer welfare prescription.'" While the tools of economics will always be essential to antitrust work, it is a disservice to the laws and their intent to retain such a laserlike focus on price effects as the measure of all that antitrust was meant to do.

But would abandoning "consumer welfare" as the lodestone of the antitrust law make the antitrust law too indeterminate? Consider the views of Judge Doug Ginsburg, who doubts that Congress really intended maximization of "consumer welfare" to be the Sherman Act's goal, but argues that the alternatives used for most of the twentieth century created too much leeway and unpredictability. As he complains, "[c]ourts were freely choosing among multiple, incommensurable, and often conflicting values."

These fears are exaggerated, for there will be a post-consumer welfare antitrust that is practicable and arguably as predictable as the consumer welfare standard. I say that in part because, in practice, the consumer welfare standard has not set a high bar. Decades of practice have shown that the promised scientific certainty of the Chicago method has not materialized, for economics does not yield answers but arguments. In practice, the consumer welfare standard asks judges and lawyers to do something nearly impossible: to measure the welfare effects of highly complex transactions or conduct. Instead, we

136   should be asking judges to do something far more suited to a legal entity. Courts should assess whether the targeted conduct is that which "promotes competition or whether it is such as may suppress or even destroy competition"—the standard prescribed by Brandeis in his *Chicago Board of Trade* opinion issued in 1918.

The "protection of competition" test is focused on protection of a *process,* as opposed to the maximization of a *value.* It is based on the premise that the legal system often does better trying to protect a process than the far more ambitious goal of maximizing an abstract value like welfare or wealth. The former asks the legal system to eliminate subversions and abuses; the latter, in contrast, inevitably demands some exercise in social planning, and ascertaining values that can be exceedingly difficult, if not impossible, to measure. Because "welfare" is so hard to ascertain, courts and enforcers rely too heavily on price effects, since they are the easiest to measure—yielding underenforcement of the law.

As a legal matter, the "protection of competition" standard has the advantage of much greater support from congressional intent and earlier precedent. It is a challenging, even absurd exercise, to pick a modern economic standard out of the language of the Sherman, Clayton, or Anti-Merger Acts or their legislative histories. The idea that Congress was concerned with "allocative efficiency" in 1890 or even 1914 or 1950 is an economic version of anthropomorphism. In contrast, it is no great stretch to say that Congress was interested in the preservation of competition. The Congressional record does not contain the words "allocative efficiency," "consumer welfare,"

or "wealth transfer," but it does repeatedly discuss the choice
between competition and monopoly. Here, as just one typical
example, is Representative Dick Thompson Morgan in 1914:
"the one thing we wish to maintain, and retain and sustain, is
competition. We want to destroy monopoly and restore and
maintain competition."

These considerations suggest a return to "protection of
competition" as the recognized goal of American antitrust law.
As scholar Barak Orbach makes clear, protection of competition was the accepted and restated goal of the antitrust laws
from the 1890s through the 1970s. The point was repeated over
the decades: In 1904 the Supreme Court said that the Sherman
Act "has prescribed the rule of free competition among those
engaged in . . . commerce." Or as it said in the 1950s, "The
heart of our national economic policy long has been faith in
the value of competition. . . . 'Congress was dealing with competition, which it sought to protect, and monopoly, which
it sought to prevent.'" And in 1978, the Court observed that
"Congress . . . sought to establish a regime of competition
as the fundamental principle governing commerce in this
country." In short, to use the "protection of competition" standard is not to break new ground but to return to what the democratic majority asked for.

Its better legal pedigree may be why some members of the
judiciary have begun to use a protection of competition standard again. Without much fanfare, Justice Stephen Breyer, in
condemning so-called "pay for delay" settlements in the pharmaceutical industry, did so based on the "potential for genuine
adverse effects on competition." Richard Posner writes that "the

138   purpose of antitrust law, at least as articulated in the modern cases, is to protect the competitive process as a means of promoting economic efficiency."

This kind of analysis attempts to capture far more of the dynamics of the competitive process than do existing analyses, and also implicates political considerations as well. As a legal matter, it marks a return to Brandeis's original "rule of reason" which was far more concerned with the competitive process. As Brandeis wrote, "[t]he true test of legality is whether the restraint imposed is such as merely regulates and perhaps thereby promotes competition or whether it is such as may suppress or even destroy competition. . . ."

The Neo-Brandesian antitrust agenda is not an agenda for solving every economic challenge produced by the new Gilded Age. But structure matters, and these suggestions would help us return to an economic vision that prizes dynamism and possibility, and ultimately attunes economic structure to a democratic society.

The English Magna Carta, the Constitution of the United States, and other foundational laws of democracies around the world were all created with the idea that power should be limited—that it should be distributed, decentralized, checked, and balanced, so that no person or institution could enjoy unaccountable influence.

Yet this vision has always had a major loophole. Written as a reaction to government tyranny, it did not contemplate the possibility of a concentrated private power that might come to rival the public's, of businesspeople with more influence than government officials, and of an artificial creature of law,

the corporation, that would grow to have political protection
exceeding that of actual humans.

That's why the struggle for democracy now and in the progressive era must be one centered on private power—in both its influence over, and union with, government. Brandeis viewed a true democracy as one composed of liberties and securities, so as to enable human flourishing in a nation of rough economic equals. It is a challenging balance to get right. But if we know one thing, it is that we are very far from a defensible division of the spoils of progress or the kind of economic security that yields human flourishing.

By providing checks on monopoly and limiting private concentration of economic power, the antitrust law can maintain and support a different economic structure than the one we have now. It can give humans a fighting chance against corporations, and free the political process from invisible government. But to turn the ship, as the leaders of the Progressive era did, will require an acute sensitivity to the dangers of the current path, the growing threats to the Constitutional order, and the potential of rebuilding a nation that actually lives up to its greatest ideals.

ACKNOWLEDGMENTS

I wish to thank Tina Bennett, who does her job better than anyone I know and whose idea it was to write a small book about bigness. Nicholas Lemann and Jimmy So provided important editorial direction, and I appreciate that Camille McDuffie and Mirada Sita really got behind this book. For comments and conversations I am grateful to Scott Hemphill, Vince Blasi (who provided Learned Hand's memories of Brandeis), Jon Sallet (another Brandeis aficionado), my wife Kate (who thought J. P. Morgan was roughly handled), Daniel Markovitz, and to Franklin Foer who also helped steer this book.

I presented an early version of the book as Stanford's Wesson Lecture and benefited greatly from the comments of readers Joshua Cohen, Lina Khan, and Reid Hoffman. I also presented it at Yale, to my Columbia colleagues, as a talk at NYU law school, and at the Roosevelt Institute. The antitrust history conference associated with the Tobin Project at the University of Michigan organized by Daniel Crane and Bill Novak provided important ideas. I am grateful to Columbia law school and dean Gillian Lester for the summer funding to complete this book.

I'm grateful to my research assistants who helped me dig deep when necessary, including Josh Obear, who was particularly helpful for the Roosevelt chapters; Sam Black, who dug deep into the economics; Tyler Lee; and Nicole Fleming. To my wife Kate for her love and tolerance. And to my daughters Sierra and Essie, "without whose never-failing sympathy and encouragement this book would have been finished in half the time."

Some readers may be interested in Brandeis's own writings. *Other People's Money* (1914) is a collection of influential essays Brandeis wrote for *Harper's* magazine. A broader collection of his speeches and essays, edited by scholar Philippa Strum, is *Brandeis on Democracy* (1995). And reading the leading biography, by Melvin Urofksy, *Louis D. Brandeis: A Life* (2009), may make you into a convert.

Earlier drafts of this book included much more material on the revival of Brandesian ideas in the later 1930s, spurred by Felix Frankfurter, his associates and mentees. A particularly good source on this topic is Ellis Hawley, *The New Deal and the Problem of Monopoly* (1966), and aficionados of the big case tradition will enjoy Spencer Weber Waller's *Thurman Arnold: A Biography* (2005). Speaking of the 1930s, the relationship between democracy, fascism, and the anti-monopoly tradition is the subject of an ongoing series by Daniel Crane at the University of Michigan. The first of his studies is *Antitrust and Democracy: A Case Study From German Fascism* (working paper 2018), and among the many books studying the link between the rise of the Third Reich and the IG Farben monopoly, I would recommend Diarmuid Jeffreys, *Hell's Cartel: IG Farben and the Making of Hitler's War Machine* (2008).

I am sometimes asked for a short introduction to the antitrust law itself, which is a bit of a tall order. There is Herbert Hovenkamp's *Principles of Antitrust* (2017), technically a "hornbook," which is thorough but not really written for a general audience. Hovenkamp's *The Antitrust Enterprise: Principle and Execution* is a worthy, non-ideological exposition and defense of contemporary antitrust. A good but tragically overpriced collection of competition policy writings is *The Making of Competition Policy, Legal and Economic Sources* (Daniel A. Crane and Herbert Hovenkamp, eds.)

For those interested in academic histories of the trust movement, I recommend Martin Sklar, *The Corporate Reconstruction of American Capitalism, 1890-1916* (1988); James Livingston, *Pragmatism and the Political Economy of Cultural Evolution* (1997); and Naomi R. Lamoreaux, *The Great Merger Movement in American Business* (1985). The classic works describing and defending the movement toward bigness are Alfred Chandler's *The Visible Hand* (1977) and *Scale and Scope* (1990). Those interested in the influence of Social Darwinian thought in the late nineteenth century will enjoy the classic *Social Darwinism in American Thought* by Richard Hofstadter. The 1912 election and the contrasting approaches of it are the subject of much writing, but an accessible and focused look at the antitrust themes of the elections is in Dan Crane's "All I Really Need to Know About Antitrust I Learned in 1912" in the *Iowa Law Review* (2015).

The best way to learn about the Chicago School of antitrust is by reading Robert Bork's *The Antitrust Paradox* (1978). Another lively read is Richard Posner's "The Chicago School of Antitrust Analysis," in volume 127 of the *University of Pennsylvania Law Review* (1979). Among the many critiques and reactions to the Chicago School are Robert Pitofsky's classic "The Political Content of Antitrust," in the same volume, and another early and influential critique of the "efficiency interpretation" of the Sherman Act is Robert Lande's "Wealth Transfers as the Original and Primary Concern of Antitrust," volume 34 of *Hastings Law Journal* (1982). A volume edited by Pitofsky, *How the Chicago School Overshot the Mark: The Effect of Conservative Economic Analysis on U.S. Antitrust* (2008) contains many of the economic critiques of Chicago antitrust.

This volume is, I'd like to think, part a broader neo-progressive revival, and more specifically, a new attention to problems of economic structure and economic justice. In legal academia, it is paired with the "rediscovery" of Constitutional political economy, where a leading work is Joseph Fishkin's and William Forbath's *The Anti-Oligarchy Constitution* (2017). The *Texas Law Review* published a symposium of works on this theme in volume 94. Among many economic works, Luigi Zingales, *A Capitalism for the People: Recapturing the Lost Genius of American Prosperity* (2012), is a worthy read.

Finally, some readers may want to read more on the specific effort to revitalize antitrust and recapture some of its lost traditions. Barry Lynn presciently broke new ground with *Cornered: The New Monopoly Capitalism and the Economics of Destruction* (2009) and went on to found the Open Markets Institute. Another earlier work is Gary L. Reback's *Free the Market!: Why Only Government Can Keep the Marketplace Competitive* (2009). Scholar Barak Orbach has written a series of articles recapturing some of the older traditions, including "The Antitrust Curse of Bigness" and "How Antitrust Lost Its Goal," in volume 81 of *Fordham Law Review* (2013).

NOTES

INTRODUCTION

15   **"the Curse of Bigness":** *Other People's Money and How the Bankers Use It*, Louis Brandeis, McClure Publications, 1914.

16   **"comprehensive charter of economic liberty":** *Northern Pacific Railroad Co. v. United States*, 356 U.S. 1 (1958) (Black, J.).

17   **"Shall the industrial policy of America":** *"Competition," Louis Brandeis, American Legal News*, January 1913 at 5.

17   **"bad history, bad policy, and bad law":** "The Political Content of Antitrust," Robert Pitofsky, *University of Pennsylvania Law Review* 127 (1979): 1051.

18   **"suppress or even destroy":** *Board of Trade of City of Chicago v. United States*, 246 U.S. 231 (1918) (Brandeis, J.).

21   **"a kingly prerogative":** 21 Cong. Rec. 2457 (1889), statement of Sen. John Sherman.

CHAPTER ONE

26   **monopoly "drives progress":** "Competition Is for Losers," Peter Thiel, *Wall Street Journal*, Sept. 12, 2014.

27   **"to clear the world of them":** *Social Statics*, Herbert Spencer, John Chapman, 1851.

28   **"The American Beauty Rose":** *The History of the Standard Oil Company*, Ida M. Tarbell, McClure, Phillips & Co., 1904.

28   **"arrest the wheels of progress":** *Trusts*, S.C.T. Dodd, 1900.

28   **"Growth of a large business":** *The Incorporation of America: Culture and Society in the Gilded Age*, Alan Trachtenberg, Hill and Wang, 2007.

29   **"Nothing less was at stake":** *The Age of Reform*, Richard Hofstadter, Knopf, 1955.

29   **"economic and political power would be decentralized":** "What Happened to the Antitrust Movement?", Richard Hofstadter, in *The Political Economy of the Sherman Act*, E. Thomas Sullivan, Oxford University Press, 1991.

30   **"equality of condition":** *Democracy in America, Volume I*, Alexis de Tocqueville, trans. Henry Reeve, Walker, 1847.

CHAPTER TWO

34   **"a pure spirit and the highest ideals":** *Louis D. Brandeis: A Life*, Melvin Urofsky, Schocken Books, 2012.

34   **an "idyllic" place:** Urofsky.

36   **"Lying and sneaking are always bad":** Urofsky.

36   **"the evils of excessive bigness":** "The New England Railroad Situation," Louis D. Brandeis, *The Boston Journal*, December 13, 1912.

148

37   **"Yellow dogs will bark and snap":** Foreword to "Opening Up New England: The New Haven Railroad's Own Story," Charles S. Mellen, *The World's Work: A History of Our Time*, vol. 25, Doubleday, Page & Co., 1913.

37   **24 deaths and 105 injuries:** "Another Wreck on the New Haven: Accidents, Risk Perception, and the Stigmatization of the New York, New Haven & Hartford Railroad, 1911-1914," Mark Aldrich, *Social Science History*, Cambridge University Press, vol. 39, no. 4, Winter 2015.

37   **"Mr. Morgan holds the gun of monopoly":** *The Fall of a Railroad Empire: Brandeis and the New Haven Merger Battle*, Henry Lee Staples and Alpheus Thomas Mason, Syracuse University Press, 1947.

37   **"the reckless and scandalous expenditure of money":** *New York, New Haven & Hartford Railroad Co.: Evidence Taken before the Interstate Commerce Commission*, U.S. Congress, Senate, 63rd Cong., 2d sess., 1914, S. Doc. 543.

38   **"We are in a position":** *Control of Corporations, Persons, and Firms Engaged in Interstate Commerce: Hearings before the Committee on Interstate Commerce*, U.S. Congress, Senate, Committee on Interstate Commerce, 62nd Cong., 1911.

39   **"the development of the individual":** *Business—A Profession*, Louis D. Brandeis, Hale, Cushman & Flint, 1933.

39   **"the true end of man":** *The Sphere and Duties of Government*, Wilhelm von Humboldt, transl. Joseph Coulthard, John Chapman, 1854.

39   **"compels us to strive":** *Business—A Profession*, Brandeis.

39   **"the 'right to life' guaranteed":** "Efficiency and Social Ideals," Louis D. Brandeis, *The Independent*, November 30, 1914.

39   **"I used to leave him":** *In the Opinion of the Court*, William Domnarski, University of Illinois Press, 1996.

40   **"Men are not free":** *Business—A Profession*, Brandeis.

41   **"far more serious":** *Other People's Money and How the Bankers Use It*, Louis D. Brandeis, F.A. Stokes, 1914.

41   **"a life so inhuman":** *The Words of Justice Brandeis*, Louis D. Brandeis, ed. Solomon Goldman, Henry Schuman, 1953.

CHAPTER THREE

45   **"tacitly acknowledged that Wall Street":** *Theodore Rex*, Edmund Morris, Random House, 2001.

46   **State of the Union speech:** William McKinley, Third Annual Message to Congress (speech, Washington, D.C., December 5, 1899), The American Presidency Project, http://www.presidency.ucsb.edu/ws/print.php?pid=29540.

47   **"This is sad, sad, very sad news"**: *Morgan: American Financier*, Jean Strouse, Random House, 1999.

47   **"Now look—that damned cowboy"**: *Theodore Rex*, Edmund Morris, Random House, 2001.

47   **"The vast individual and corporate fortunes"**: Theodore Roosevelt, "National Duties" (speech, Minnesota, September 2, 1901), Almanac of Theodore Roosevelt, http://www.theodore-roosevelt.com/images/research/txtspeeches/678.pdf.

48   **"In my judgment"**: *Theodore Rex*, Edmund Morris, Random House, 2001.

49   **"When aggregated wealth demands"**: "The Progressives, Past and Present," Theodore Roosevelt, *The Outlook*, September 3, 1910.

49   **"the absolutely vital question"**: *The Republicans: A History of the Grand Old Party*, Lewis L. Gould, Random House, 2003.

49   **account of Morgan's reaction:** *Morgan: American Financier*, Jean Strouse, Random House, 1999.

50   **"a man of great wealth who does not"**: Theodore Roosevelt, "Speech at Providence, Rhode Island," (1902), in *Addresses and Presidential Messages of Theodore Roosevelt* (Knickerbocker Press, 1904).

51   **"The President of the United States"**: *Theodore Rex*, Edmund Morris, Random House, 2001.

52   **"slavery that would result from aggregations"**: *Standard Oil Co. v. United States*, 221 U.S. 1 (1911) (Harlan, J., concurring in part and dissenting in part).

52   **"placed the control of the two roads"**: *Northern Securities Co. v. United States*, 193 U.S. 197 (1904) (Harlan, J.)

53   **"it was the ferocious extreme"**: *Northern Securities Co. v. United States*, 193 U.S. 197 (1904) (Holmes, J. dissenting)

53   **"it was imperative"**: *Theodore Roosevelt: An Autobiography*, Edmund Morris, Macmillan Company, 1913.

53   **"there are great wastes in competition"**: Oliver Wendell Holmes Jr. to Frederick Pollock, May 25, 1906, in *Holmes-Pollock Letters*, ed. Mark D. Howe (Belknap Press, 1961).

54   **"power that controls the economy"**: *United States v. Columbia Steel Co.*, 334 U.S. 495 (1948) (Douglas, J., dissenting).

54   **"threat to other values"**: *Brown Shoe Co. v. United States*, 370 U.S. 294 (1962).

55   **"excessive concentration of economic power"**: "The Political Content of Antitrust," Robert Pitofsky, *University of Pennsylvania Law Review* 127 (1979): 1051.

150   58   **"tend to tilt toward the wishes of corporations"**: "Testing Theories of American Politics: Elites, Interest Groups, and Average Citizens," Martin Gilens and Benjamin I. Page, *Perspectives on Politics* 12 (2014): 3.

59   **"was like a general who"**: "John D. Rockefeller, A Character Sketch," Ida Tarbell, *McClure's Magazine*, July 1905.

60   **"'But we don't want to sell'"**: *The History of the Standard Oil Company*, Ida Tarbell, Macmillan Company, 1904.

61   **"there was no more faithful baptist"**: *The History of the Standard Oil Company*, Ida Tarbell, Macmillan Company, 1904.

61   **"A man always has two reasons"**: *The House of Morgan: An American Banking Dynasty and the Rise of Modern Finance*, Ron Chernow, Atlantic Monthly Press, 1990.

62   **"his party included, characteristically"**: *The Great Pierpont Morgan: A Biography*, Frederick L. Allen, Harper & Row, 1949.

63   **"we grudge no man"**: Theodore Roosevelt, "New Nationalism" (speech, Osawatomie, Kansas, August 31, 1910), Teaching American History, http:// teachingamericanhistory.org/ library/document/new-nationalism-speech/.

67   **"All who recall the condition"**: *Standard Oil Co. v. United States*, 221 U.S. 1 (1911)

(Harlan, J., concurring in part and dissenting in part).

71   **"It's unusual to find"**: *The Luckiest Guy in the World*, T. Boone Pickens, Beard Books, 2000.

71   **"Managers have incentives"**: "Agency Costs of Free Cash Flow, Corporate Finance, and Takeovers," Michael Jensen, *American Economic Review* 76 (May 1986): 323.

75   **"to give the National Government"**: Theodore Roosevelt, "The Trusts, the People, and the Square Deal," reprinted in *Theodore Roosevelt: An Autobiography*, Macmillan Company, 1913.

75   **"Monopoly is certain and sure"**: "A Study of Competition," Eugene Debs, *Appeal to Reason*, May 28, 1910.

CHAPTER FOUR

78   **"the problems of distribution of power within society"**: "Private Action—The Strongest Pillar of Antitrust," Lee Loevinger, *Antitrust Bulletin*, 1958.

78   **"antitrust almost as a secular religion"**: "Lee Loevinger, 91, Kennedy-Era Antitrust Chief," John Files, *The New York Times*, May 8, 2004.

79   **"the post-War currents of democracy-enhancing antitrust ideology"**: "Antitrust and Democracy: A Case Study from German Facism," Daniel A. Crane,

Law and Economics Working Papers, University of Michigan Law School, April 2018.

79   **"a Fuehrer was inevitable"**: *Business as a System of Power*, Robert Brady, Routledge, 2017.

80   **I.G. Farben chemical cartel:** *Hell's Cartel: IG Farben and the Making of Hitler's War Machine*, Diarmuid Jeffreys, Henry Holt and Company, 2010; see also, "Antitrust and Democracy: A Case Study from German Facism," Daniel A. Crane, Law and Economics Working Papers, University of Michigan Law School, April 2018.

80   **"monopolies soon got control of Germany"**: 95 Cong. Rec. 11 (1949).

80   **"a colossal empire serving the German state"**: *Elimination of German Resources for War: Hearings Before a Subcomm. of Military Affairs*, 79th Cong. 941 (1945).

81   **"what sort of country we want to live in"**: 96 Cong. Rec. 16452 (1950).

82   **efforts to transplant U.S. antitrust laws to Japan:** *Competition Law and Policy in Japan and the EU*, Etsuko Kameoka, Edward Elgar Publishing, 2014.

83   **"not a single American-trained economist of any prominence"**: *The Antitrust Experiment in America*, Donald Dewey, Columbia University Press, 1990.

83   **"now runs its quiet course"**: *The Paranoid Style in American Politics*, Richard Hofstadter, Vintage Books, 2008.

84   **"a private, competitive enterprise economy"**: "The Case Against Big Business," George J. Stigler, *Fortune*, May 1, 1952.

84   **iconoclastic economist Joseph Schumpeter:** *Capitalism, Socialism and Democracy*, Joseph A. Schumpeter, Routledge, 1976.

84   **"did not take seriously the problems"**: *The Master Switch: The Rise and Fall of Information Empires*, Tim Wu, Vintage Books, 2011.

85   **"the existing structure is the efficient structure"**: *In Defense of Industrial Concentration*, John S. McGee, Praeger, 1971.

87   **"destroyed my dreams of socialism"**: "Aaron Director, Economist, Dies at 102," Douglas Martin, *The New York Times*, Sept. 16, 2004.

88   **"only that value we would today call consumer welfare"**: "Legislative Intent and the Policy of the Sherman Act," Robert H. Bork, *Journal of Law and Economics*, 1966.

89   **" a kingly prerogative"**: *Trusts*, Speech by John Sherman to the U.S. Senate, 1890.

89   **"Bork's analysis of the legislative history was strained"**: "Antitrust's Protected Classes," Herbert Hovenkamp, *Michigan Law Review*, 1989.

89   **"prefer a system of small producers"**: *United States v.*

152   *Aluminum Co. of Am.*, 148 F.2d 416
(2d Cir. 1945).

90   **"a value will be announced
as pertinent":** "Legislative Intent
and the Policy of the Sherman Act,"
Robert H. Bork, *Journal of Law and
Economics*, 1966.

91   **"oversimplified economics":**
"Antitrust Made (Too) Simple,"
Christopher R. Leslie, *Antitrust
Law Journal*, 2014.

CHAPTER FIVE

94   **"unless the would-be
monopolist":** *The Industrial
Reorganization Act: Hearings before
the Subcommittee on Antitrust and
Monopoly*, U.S. Congress, Senate,
Committee on the Judiciary, 93rd
Cong., 2d sess., 1974.

94   **"The vicious acts
associated":** "Public Utilities and
Public Policy," Theodore N. Vail, *The
Atlantic Monthly*, Volume 111, 1913.

95   **"must have absolute
control":** In the Matter of Use of the
Carterfone Device, 13 F.C.C.2d 420
(1968).

98   **"where I think there is a
case":** "Joel Klein, Hanging Tough,"
David Segal, *The Washington Post*,
March 24, 1998.

98   **"in a secret memo":** "The
Internet Tidal Wave," Bill Gates, May
26, 1995.

CHAPTER SIX

103   **His citation: "R. Bork":**
Reiter v. Sonotone Corp., 442 U.S. 330
(1979) (Burger, C.J.).

104   **"sheriff of a frontier town":**
The Antitrust Paradox, Robert Bork,
Free Press, 1978.

104   **"The persistent dominance
of an industry":** "Dominant Firms
and the Monopoly Problem: Market
Failure Considerations," Oliver E.
Williamson, *Harvard Law Review* 85
(1972): 1512.

105   **it was the Harvard school
that quietly:** *Antitrust Law: An
Analysis of Antitrust Principles and
Their Application*, Philip Areeda and
Donald Turner, Little, Brown and
Company (1978).

105   **"grafted economic
thinking":** "The Influence of the
Areeda-Hovenkamp Treatise in the
Lower Courts and What It Means for
Institutional Reform in Antitrust,"
Rebecca H. Allensworth. *Iowa Law
Review* 100 (2015): 1919.

108   **Thomas Krattenmaken and
Steven Salop:** "Anticompetitive
Exclusion: Raising Rivals' Costs
to Achieve Power Over Price,"
Thomas G. Krattenmaker and
Steven C. Salop, *Yale Law Journal* 96
(1986): 209.

108   **Carl Shapiro:** "Navigating
the Patent Thicket: Cross Licenses,
Patent Pools, and Standard Setting,"
Carl Shapiro, *Innovation Policy and
the Economy* 1 (2001): 119.

108   **Michael L. Katz and Howard A. Shelanski:** "Mergers and Innovation," Michael L. Katz and Howard A. Shelanski, *Antitrust Law Journal* 74 (2007): 1.

108   **Jon Baker:** "Exclusion as a Core Competition Concern," Jonathan B. Baker, 78 *Antitrust Law Journal* (2012): 527.

108   **Daniel Rubenfeld:** See, e.g., "Quantitative Methods in Antitrust," Daniel L. Rubinfeld, *Issues in Competition Law and Policy* 1 (2008): 723.

108   **"because extreme interpretations":** *How Chicago Overshot the Mark: The Effect of Conservative Economic Analysis On U.S. Antitrust Policy*, Robert Pitofsky, Oxford University Press, 2008.

109   **"The mere possession of monopoly power":** *Verizon Communications Inc. v. Law Offices of Curtis V. Trinko, LLP*, 540 U.S. 398 (2004) (Scalia, J.).

111   **"a farce of such mindboggling proportions":** *Building IBM: Shaping an Industry and Its Technology*, Emerson W. Pugh, MIT Press, 1995.

114   **"trustbusting is the Sherman Act's most alluring":** "Failed Expectations: The Troubled Past and Uncertain Future of the Sherman Act as a Tool for Deconcentration," William E. Kovacic, *Iowa Law Review* 74 (1989): 1105.

114   **"the evils of Monopoly are largely independent":** *Antitrust Law: An Analysis of Antitrust*

Principles and Their Application, Philip Areeda and Donald Turner, Little, Brown and Company (1978).

115   **A full 75 percent of industries:** "Are US Industries Becoming More Concentrated?" Gustavo Grullon et al. (2015), available at http://finance.eller .arizona.edu/sites/finance/files/ grullon_11.4.16.pdf.

115   **studies by the Council of Economic Advisors:** "Benefits of Competition and Indicators of Market Power," Council of Economic Advisors Issue Brief (2016), available at https://obamawhitehouse. archives.gov/sites/default/ files/page/files/20160414_cea_ competition_issue_brief.pdf.

115   **an independent study by the *Economist*:** "Corporate Concentration," *The Economist*, March 24, 2016.

115   **The OECD, in its own:** "Market Concentration," OECD Issues paper by the Secretariat (2018), available at https://one. oecd.org/document/DAF/COMP/ WD(2018)46/en/pdf.

117   **"an antitrust division in the Justice Department":** Barack Obama (speech, Oregon, May 18, 2008), *Reuters*.

CHAPTER SEVEN

119   **"imagine a place where trespassers leave no footprints":** "Electronic Frontier: Coming Into the Country," John Perry Barlow,

154   *Communications of the ACM*,
January 1991.

122   **Instagram "allows people
to do what they like to do on
Facebook":** "Instagram Was
Facebook's Biggest Threat," Nicholas
Carlson, *Business Insider*, April 9,
2012.

122   **"Buying Instagram conveyed
to investors":** "Here's Proof
that Instagram Was One of the
Smartest Acquisitions Ever," Victor
Luckerson, *TIME*, April 19, 2016.

124   **"the most popular
messaging app":** "A Year Later,
$19 Billion for WhatsApp Doesn't
Sound So Crazy," Josh Constine,
TechCrunch, Feb. 19, 2015.

124   **"Without this acquisition":**
"Facebook's WhatsApp Acquisition
Exposes Grave Risks to the Business
Model," *Seeking Alpha*, Feb. 20,
2014.

126   **"monopoly profits":**
"Competition Is for Losers," Peter
Thiel, *Wall Street Journal*, Sept. 12,
2014.

126   **"bringing the world closer
together":** "Facebook Careers,"
Facebook.

126   **"different kind of company":**
"Facebook Careers," various job
postings, Facebook.

CONCLUSION

127   **"a barrier to what Congress
saw was the rising tide of economic
concentration":** *Brown Shoe Co. v.
United States*, 370 U.S. 294 (1962).

129   **same institutional owners:**
"Anticompetitive Effects of Common
Ownership," José Azar, Martin C.
Schmalz, and Isabel Tecu, *Journal of
Finance*, August 2018.

135   **"multiple,
incommensurable, and often
conflicting values":** "Bork's
'Legislative Intent' and the Courts,"
Douglas H. Ginsburg, *Antitrust Law
Journal*, 2014.

137   **"the one thing we wish
to maintain":** 51 Cong. Rec. 9265
(1914).

137   **"prescribed the rule of free
competition":** *N. Sec. Co. v. United
States*, 193 U.S. 197 (1904).

137   **"the heart of our national
economic policy":** *Standard Oil Co.
v. Fed. Trade Comm'n*, 340 U.S. 231
(1951).

137   **"the fundamental principle
governing commerce":** *City of
Lafayette, La. v. Louisiana Power &
Light Co.*, 435 U.S. 389 (1978).

137   **"genuine adverse effects on
competition":** *F.T.C. v. Actavis, Inc.*,
570 U.S. 136 (2013).

138   **"as a means of promoting
economic efficiency":** *Morrison v.
Murray Biscuit Co.*, 797 F.2d 1430 (7th
Cir. 1986).

138   **"true test of legality":** *Bd.
of Trade of City of Chicago v. United
States*, 246 U.S. 231 (1918).

Columbia Global Reports is a publishing imprint from Columbia University that commissions authors to do original on-site reporting around the globe on a wide range of issues. The resulting novella-length books offer new ways to look at and understand the world that can be read in a few hours. Most readers are curious and busy. Our books are for them.

Subscribe to Columbia Global Reports and get six books a year in the mail in advance of publication. globalreports.columbia.edu/subscribe